Sowing, reaping, keeping

Sowing, reaping, keeping

People-sensitive evangelism

Laurence Singlehurst

CROSSWAY BOOKS
Leicester

ISBN 1–85684–052–2

Unless otherwise stated, quotations from the Bible are from
the Revised Standard Version, copyrighted 1946, 1952, ©
1971, 1973, by the Division of Christian Education,
National Council of the Churches of Christ in the USA, and
used by permission.

Typeset by Avocet Type, Brill, Aylesbury, Bucks.

Printed in Great Britain for Crossway Books,
38 De Montfort Street, Leicester LE1 7GP,
by Cox & Wyman Ltd, Reading, Berkshire.

Contents

Foreword

Reading this book reminded me of the man who asked the question, 'How do you eat an elephant?' He thought carefully for a moment and then replied, 'In bite-sized chunks.'

We know as Christians that we should be active in sharing our faith, but the thought of influencing our nation, our neighbourhood or even our best friend towards a living relationship with Jesus Christ is, for many of us, about as realistic as eating an elephant.

Here is a book that takes a down-to-earth, bite-sized chunks approach. Laurence Singlehurst taps into a rich seam of experience to provide some useful insights that will be of help to individual Christians, housegroups, local church leaders – in fact anyone who is concerned about sharing their faith intelligently and effectively.

He rightly emphasises the twin importance of strategic thinking and informed prayer, and alongside these develops ways in which 'sowing, reaping and keeping' principles can be applied.

Here is a book that moves beyond the theory of evangelism to its practice. Because of that, and the scale of the task we face, it is a book we all need to read.

Ian Coffey
Senior Minister; Mutley Baptist Church,
Plymouth, England,
January, 1995

Acknowledgments

In writing a book like this one wants to thank a whole host of people but I would particularly like to thank all the fellow YWAMers that I have worked alongside and learnt lessons from over twenty years. Special thanks to Rachel Ellis who typed the manuscript, to Andrew Wooding who made my English real English, to James Featherby, my friend and critical reader of early manuscripts, to Alistair and the River Church who have faithfully supported and encouraged me.

A very special thank you to Ailish, my wonderful Irish wife, and patient children.

1

A clearer understanding

Evangelism – those who know Jesus, telling those who don't know him.

I am sure we all agree that this is something Christians are called to do. It may even be that you are eager and ready to do it. But have any of you in recent years come away from an evangelistic endeavour feeling bitterly disappointed? Most, if not all, of you can probably answer 'Yes' to this. I certainly can! So, why is it that something so potentially exciting and faith-building can be such a common source of frustration?

Let me put it to you that most of the disappointment we feel is of our own making. This is because we think we understand what evangelism is, but more often we do not.

In this book I want to explore a new understanding of evangelism for the nineties so that we no longer suffer from constant disappointment and can begin to see the results that all of us long for.

Mountain climbing

The experience of many churches looks like this. They put a great deal of effort into coming up with an idea for outreach into the community. They, as it were, climb a mountain (carry through the idea). But at the end of all their hard work and climbing, they plunge into a valley of disappointment because their expectations were just not met.

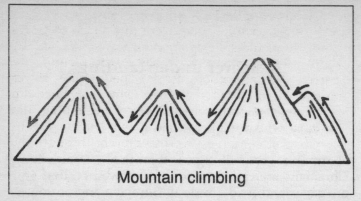

Mountain climbing

Then, because the church is agreed that evangelism is something they definitely must do, again they scale the mountain and again they plummet into the valley of disappointment. They try a further time and perhaps see the results they originally hoped for and think that they have cracked it. Then they repeat their idea and this time it fails. Finally, they try out an idea that they are convinced will not work, and it does.

Why?

Spanish experience

My own experience in twenty years of evangelism is very much like this: seeing some things work and at other times being frustrated for no apparent reason.

I particularly remember one outreach where we were convinced that the latest solution to our evangelistic problems lay in us having more faith and power.

An evangelist friend and I were running a short discipleship course in England for Youth With A Mission. We spent three whole months pumping the expectations of the students, building them up in faith and encouraging them to believe God for the power of the Holy Spirit in evangelism.

All of us on the course were due to go to Spain where we would split up into four teams. We had the whole outreach planned. We had learnt a handful of Spanish-language choruses. We had some clever mimed dramas prepared. Each team was lined up with an expert interpreter. We were going to go into the Spanish town squares, sing our songs, do our dramas, gather large crowds, preach through the interpreters, and the power of God would come down and many would be saved. Wouldn't they?

Anyway, soon we were off to Spain with the faith that we would see at least one hundred Spaniards become Christians through our efforts. Never had a team left with so much expectation that God would move.

One team arrived in Northern Spain in a little town called Fugares, a tremendous buzz of excitement amongst them and their faith running high. Off they set immediately to what they were sure would be the busy town square. Unfortunately, they had not realised that Fugares nestled at the bottom of the Pyrenees mountains and, in the month of November, a freezing wind blows past the glaciers of the Pyrenees and right through the middle of town.

The team leader knew something was wrong when they arrived at the square and found that even the sparrows had their scarves on. However, they preached and sang with gusto, even though the square was empty. But the only interesting thing that happened was that the guitarist's aching fingers turned a nasty shade of blue.

The team leader, sensibly realising that open-air evangelism wasn't quite the course of action for them, knew he had to find something for his team to do for the rest of the month. So he had a blinding flash of revelation and told them that they would be the prayer team of the outreach and the expected revival would happen with the other teams. Being good students, they swallowed all this and assailed the heavenlies with their prayers.

All was well until the team leader telephoned one of the other teams where Alan, the overall leader for the outreach, was based. Before our team leader could say anything, Alan jumped in with: 'I have something important to say: my team is the prayer team and it's all going to happen with your team.'

'No,' cried our team leader, '*my* team is the prayer team!'

A month later the outreach to Spain was over and the four teams were reunited on the boat back to England. The leaders, glad to see each other again, compared notes on their experiences. Much to their horror they realised that no one during the outreach had come to know the Lord, and each of the four teams had spent the whole month in prayer.

Our team leader to Fugares spent the rest of the sea-crossing hiding from his students as he could not explain to them why all the exciting conversions he had promised them hadn't happened.

The next year this leader led another team to Spain. Learning from the previous fiasco, he insisted to his team beforehand: 'No one is going to be saved during this outreach – all we are going to do is pray.' And with this in mind, he set off to Spain once more with his students.

On the first night of the outreach his team had led ten people to the Lord. And by the end of the outreach they had planted a church.

Confused? So was the team leader!

Training

Here is another of the many confusing stories I could tell you!

About ten years ago I did a series of evangelism training courses with five local churches, giving the same training to each of them. Two of those churches put their training into action and doubled in size; two put their training into action and nothing happened at all; and the last church did the same and disappeared entirely! *With the same training!*

So what was the reason?

Knowing the way

After all my various experiences I cried out to God that I needed to understand more about evangelism. Why did some attempts work and others fail miserably? When reading my Bible, verse 7 of Psalm 103 stood out as if in answer to my prayer.

This verse tells us that the children of Israel saw the *acts* of God, but Moses *knew* the way to God. It struck me forcibly then that I had seen the acts of God (many people saved in the work I'd been involved in), but I still needed to understand God's ways in the area of evangelism. I promptly applied myself to much Bible study and thinking.

In the last twenty years we have seen God do great things in the church. We have had a new understanding of worship, of team leadership, and of the whole of the body of Christ being involved in the work of the church. We have been given a new love for fellowship, a greater understanding of prayer, and many other vital lessons that have added to the vibrancy of the church and equipped us for the nineties.

13

However, I would suggest that in the area of evangelism we have not had a fresh understanding. I am afraid we still do the same old things the same old ways. Tom Sine, the well-known futurist, has said that Christians so often plan for tomorrow to be like today. Our world has changed – has our evangelism?

In the following chapters I want to explore the conclusions that I developed from my own research, and also from the experience of others.

Both sides of Paul's ministry

When starting my research, the first part of the Bible I looked into was the book of Acts, particularly the chapters showing the ministry of the Apostle Paul.

When studying these chapters before, what had really leapt out at me, and what many people were teaching on, was the supernatural aspect of his ministry. If we look at the last twenty years, the work of the Holy Spirit has been stressed more than anything else in the church. Amongst other things, this has led to a real emphasis on personal revelation, or hearing from God. Many of us, myself included, have swung out into this aspect of ministry.

On the other side, however, there must be an emphasis on the Bible, as well as the seemingly non-spiritual aspects of principles and strategy which in themselves are biblical.

I came to know the Lord through 'Jesus freaks' – those from the hippy generation who were fanatical about Jesus – and we were so into personal revelation that we had prayer meetings to know if we should wake up in the morning, followed by other prayer meetings to make similar menial decisions.

But when looking through the book of Acts, not only did I see an emphasis on the Holy Spirit – I also

14

began to see the emphasis on strategy. It was clear that the Apostle Paul had a strategy for his work, and it was not just revelation-based.

In every place Paul went to, except Athens and Lystra, his ministry followed a similar pattern. Most places he went to he found Jews first, or if not then he found a group of God-fearers. Now why did this apostle to the Gentiles go to the Jews first? We could put forward all sorts of arguments, such as 'Perhaps he felt an obligation to the Jews.' But maybe there is a more simple explanation. That actually the Jews were the easiest people to reach. First, they understood the basic concepts of God (the Christian gospel, of course, is based on Judaic beliefs). Secondly, they were from a similar culture to Paul himself. This means that they spoke the same language as he did, they shared many of the same cultural normatives, and therefore there was no cross-cultural bridge for the Apostle Paul to reach these displaced Jews. If we are reaching people of a similar culture to ourselves, who speak the same language as we do, they are in all probability easier to reach.

So could we not draw the conclusion that the Apostle Paul had a strategy to meet the easiest people so that they would become his resource base to reaching the people around them? They understood the culture of the nation they were living in; they understood the local language and dialect; and they were committed long term to that particular location. It's common sense!

Strategy

We could ask ourselves the same question. Do we have a strategy for reaching the easiest people around us? Would we even know who the easiest people were?

15

The first principle we want to think about in evangelism in the nineties and the first step of our new understanding, is that we must hold a tension between the Holy Spirit and revelation on one side, and the Scriptures and strategic planning on the other.

Let me tell you this: it is not worldly to use our minds. We can use our gifts of intelligence and understanding to think and plan what might be the best way to reach our community with the gospel. It is not worldly for a church to have a two-year plan in some detail, a five-year plan in outline, and even some thoughts way into the future. I have visited many churches over the years, but I have not found one that had a written-out plan of how they could reach their community. Most were working on the latest thing they felt God was saying to them.

As we will show in chapters two and three, perhaps we fail to understand totally what God is saying to us because we do not see it in the bigger picture.

Am I saying that we should abandon the Holy Spirit and rely only on strategies? No. We need both. And when we have developed our plan using minds God has given us and principles that we have learned from Scripture, we will then need to call on the Holy Spirit to give us creative ideas in the implementing of it. Our strategies from the very beginning can come out of our prayer and our hearing from God, and we then should develop them using the wisdom that God has given us.

If we are going to make specific headway in reaching our nation in the nineties, we must grasp this issue further. As churches and as individuals, we have to be prepared to live in this tension.

2

What is evangelism?

One cause of confusion in modern-day evangelism is Christians not understanding what evangelism is in the first place. Quite a problem, as you can see.

As soon as we say the word 'evangelism' certain pictures leap into our minds. Maybe images of people banging on doors and being greeted with: 'We're not interested in the Mormons, thank you!' Or some dedicated individual standing on a street corner preaching his or her heart out to no one in particular.

If we ask ourselves 'What is evangelism?', we could write down a very nice list of:

● Living the Christlike life
● Doing the good works that God has called us to
● Preaching and being good news to those around us
● Proclaiming the gospel message
● Seeing people make decisions for Christ

And our list could go on.

But it is my firm belief that our understanding (or rather, *mis*understanding) of what evangelism really involves is one of the greatest problems facing the church today. Even though we can all agree on the list I have written above, most evangelicals in their hearts believe something different. There is a disparity between our conscious and our subconscious definition of what evangelism is. Most of us are driven by our subconscious definition. Which of course begs the question: what *is* our subconscious definition?

If we were to ask an average group of evangelical Christians whether they have come away from their experience of evangelism with a sense of disappointment, my research and that of others shows that over seventy per cent would respond with a resounding 'Yes!' It is my conviction that the average church members' disappointment is the greatest hindrance to our evangelism today. And if people are disappointed, both their energy and their motivation are sapped.

When we ask people *why* they are disappointed, the number one response is that they have seen no one saved or make a decision for Christ. Their second reason is that their expectations were not met. And the third reason is that they are disappointed in themselves.

In other words, people's subconscious definition of evangelism is seeing people saved. They are looking for some form of result, and it is this that causes the problem. It needn't, because evangelism is *not* simply seeing people saved.

'What?' you cry. But don't call out the heresy police just yet. You see, I do believe that seeing people saved is a *part* of evangelism.

Let me further explore this by asking two more pertinent questions: 'What are the problems in thinking that evangelism is seeing people saved?' and 'What is evangelism?'

The Engle scale

1 — 2 — 3 — 4 — 5 — 6 — 7 — 8 — 9 —10

Let us look at a scale from one to ten (sometimes

called the Engle scale after the man who first used it in this context) and take point one as people with a negative picture of God, and points nine to ten as people accepting Christ and becoming Christians.

If we were to go out and ask people in our town what they think God is like, the sort of replies we would get would be:

'I don't believe in him.'

'God is a force.'

'He's not just, he doesn't care.'

'He's like Father Christmas.'

Basically, we would get a very negative picture.

And if we asked what people thought of the church today, we would get an even more negative picture: 'Christians are boring, hypocrites, narrow minded, fundamentalists, religious fanatics', and so on.

Where would you say most of the population is on this scale? Right – the bottom!

Sadly, one of the most fundamental factors which affects evangelism today is that an increasing proportion of the population is at the bottom end of this scale. In recent times we have probably never experienced an age like ours where there has been such a negative picture of God – and it is extremely important that we recognise this.

If we look back to thirty years ago, and certainly before the Second World War, we see that far more people in Britain went to church or Sunday School. Therefore, they had at least a partially accurate picture of what God is really like and hopefully what Christians are really like as well. Obviously, the story is very different now.

19

Pushing up the scale

Let us take this thought to its next stage. If our subconscious understanding of evangelism is result-focused (the result being seeing people give their lives to Jesus), then how has that affected the way we have evangelised in the last twenty years? It has meant that a great deal of our evangelism, whether it is preaching at meetings or street work, has been aimed simply at asking people to make a decision for Christ.

We talk to people as if they have a positive picture of God already. But in fact they don't. It is almost as if we are asking them to give their lives to a monster and join the most boring group of people on the face of the earth. No wonder they tell us, 'No!'

So what really is evangelism? It is meeting people at whatever point they are at on the scale and, through that encounter, their picture of God and of the church is changed. Through this change, step by step, they see that the gospel message is good news for them and relevant to their situation.

So if someone moves from step one to step two, that is evangelism, and likewise if someone goes from point five to point eight. And if we take someone from step eight to step ten and lead them to Christ, that is evangelism as well. As you know, whenever someone does that, we call that person the evangelist, get ever so excited and put a crown on his or her head. In doing that we are sending out the message that everyone else is a failure and the person that led our convert to the Lord is the only successful evangelist.

So we can see that our definition of evangelism is extremely important. Every Christian needs to have the same definition, both conscious and subconscious, that evangelism is a process, over a period of time, of taking people from where they are and changing their picture of God and the church. Through the work of the Holy Spirit, they will then hopefully want to give their lives to Christ.

Sowing and reaping

I want to introduce two words to this process and say that evangelism is a 'sowing' and a 'reaping' process. As we see in John 4:34–38:

> Jesus said to them, 'My food is to do the will of him who sent me, and to accomplish his work. Do you not say, "There are yet four months, then comes the harvest"? I tell you, lift up your eyes, and see how the fields are already white for harvest. He who reaps receives wages, and gathers fruit for eternal life, so that sower and reaper may rejoice together. For here the saying holds true, "One sows and another reaps." I sent you to reap that for which you did not labour; others have laboured, and you have entered into their labour.'

From this passage comes much of the teaching on evangelism that we have traditionally heard. However, Jesus concludes it with an interesting point.

He talks about the sower and the reaper working together – one sows, the other reaps. Of course, what he is talking about is what the prophets of old had sowed into the Samaritan people. They believed in one God, and they were expecting a Messiah and a Saviour. So the fundamentals were sown into the 'woman at the well' even though she was leading an immoral life. So when Jesus revealed himself as the Messiah to her he was able to reap her into the kingdom.

This concept of sowing and reaping is an extremely important one. As I go round more and more churches and look at the different situations that exist I see that as the body of Christ gets more enthusiastic about evangelism (which is good), the strategies that we tend to adopt are only reaping ones (which is not good).

Let me put it this way: if you saw a farmer go out into a field with a combine harvester expecting to reap his field without first taking the rocks from it, without it being ploughed, without any seed being planted in the first place, but he was *still* hoping for a harvest, you would think he was one bale short of a load. And quite rightly too. But isn't this what a lot of our evangelism is like?

Many evangelists have gone to churches to hold missions and, in my opinion, are expected to be magicians. Somehow this evangelist is meant to attract non-Christians who have never previously darkened the door of the church, and they are meant to respond in their hundreds to the altar call. When this does not happen, the poor person is blamed for being a bad evangelist.

But if we see evangelism as both a sowing and a reaping process, many of our evangelism strategies will begin to make sense. If we are going to allow a church mission to invite an evangelist, it really should be as part of a strategy. The church should have spent the previous year sowing into the community, building relationships, getting to know non-Christians, and demonstrating the wonder and love of Jesus Christ in many attractive ways, so that when we have that mission we can reap in the hard work that we have previously sown.

Great expectations

This 'sowing and reaping' definition of evangelism is also extremely important for our expectations. As we have already seen, disappointment is a huge hindrance to effective evangelism. And one of the major areas that causes disappointment is that we in the body of Christ have *reaping* expectations of *sowing* strategies.

Let me give you one example. I went to a country church that had been running a little restaurant in the nearby town. The day before I arrived they had closed the restaurant down. When I asked the leaders why, they said that it had been a failure. I asked them what they meant by this, and they explained that it was a failure because they had only seen four converts in five years.

In my normal tactful fashion I replied, 'Oh, it wasn't a failure, it was a success!' This did not engender a positive response, so I went on to ask the following questions: 'Was the restaurant well used?'

'Yes!' they cried. 'It was full most days!'

'How many people, do you think, through coming to your restaurant saw Christians in a more positive light?'

'Oh, thousands,' they replied.

And when I asked them how many people did they think saw *God* in a more positive light, 'hundreds and hundreds' was their reply.

So, in other words, it was a wonderful sowing strategy but not such a good reaping one, which is hardly a surprise.

We can see from this illustration that not only did this church suffer from unnecessary disappointment, but they had also begun to doubt whether God had spoken to them about opening the restaurant in the first place. If we have reaping expectations of a sowing strategy then of course we will be doomed to disappointment. It is inevitable.

I could go on to relate how countless other churches have suffered in the same way: such as thriving mother and toddler groups that were closed because no one was saved, and yet mother and toddler groups are an excellent sowing strategy.

I was involved in another church that at great expense had rented the largest theatre in town and put on an ambitious Christmas pantomime. The theatre was full to capacity, and every night over sixty per cent of the audience were non-Christians. Yet at the end of their run the church was devastated because no one in the audience had actually been converted. Once again we can see that this was a great sowing strategy, but they had expected the results of a reaping one. No wonder they were disappointed.

The other side of the coin is that some churches have sowing strategies with no reaping expectations. They work on good relational-based ideas, but have not thought through how they can be taken from a sowing strategy through to one of reaping.

One-on-one

We can also see how our expectations affect our one-to-one relationships. Because of our misunderstanding of sowing and reaping, we have a tendency to expect too much too quickly. So it is essential that we understand the process that people have to go through before they can make a proper decision for Christ.

When you meet a new friend, imagine that you form a relationship bridge with that person, and let us say that it has a one ton capacity. What we often do is drive our five ton gospel truck over our one ton relationship bridge, and of course we all know what happens: the bridge breaks and the relationship collapses. You can see this on the following illustration.

So what should we do? Well, perhaps it would be better for us to recognise that we have a formative relationship and to break down our five ton gospel message, as it were, into five one ton messages. Then,

over a period of time, we can put them across.

If we only see evangelism as leading people to the Lord, we will find this very difficult, but if we have accepted that evangelism is a sowing and reaping process we won't have any problem in taking our time.

Research has shown that most people who come to know the Lord first of all need five to seven positive experiences of Christianity. Once we accept this idea, it takes all the pressure out of our evangelism and everyone can feel a part of the process. Many people by personality are much better equipped at building relationships, and through their everyday lives and the words they share can show the reality of their Christian experience. Then in the right time and in the right place they can invite their friends into a situation where they can hear more of the content of the gospel and have an opportunity to respond to it.

Wrong assumptions

At this point many people will cry, 'What if we only have this one opportunity? Surely we must give the whole gospel now. What if they get run over tomorrow?' And they will quote scriptures that God's word will not return to him void.

We make several assumptions here that we need to consider. Perhaps we have the misguided idea that we ourselves are solely responsible for this evangelism process. However, the Scriptures show us that the eye of God searches to and fro across the earth looking for any that might turn to him. In other words, *God* is in charge of the evangelism process and I believe that *our* goal is to leave people positive for the next Holy Spirit encounter.

I remember watching a number of young people

who were 'all out' for evangelism, and were very much on fire and excited about their faith. Three men were talking to a very small eighty-year-old lady with a walking frame. They were explaining to her in great depth the entire gospel, from Genesis to Revelation, with a particular emphasis on how long she might spend in the hell-fires. I stepped into this situation, grabbed hold of the lady, took her out of the crowd, and asked her who all those horrible people were.

'I don't know, sonny,' she said to me. Well, praise God for that! I then spent a wonderful half-hour talking with her, bought her a cup of tea and within the context of that was able to share just a little bit about Christianity and left her very positive for that next Holy Spirit encounter.

Do I believe in street evangelism? The answer is: yes, very much, and in later chapters we will explore in detail how to be effective in street work. But whether it is in our own personal relationships, on the doors, or out on the streets, we must remember that it is more important to leave people positive than to give them everything we know.

So, what about the thought that God's word will not go back to him void? I think when *God* speaks, this will always be the case. His voice will always bring forth fruit. But we humans are at best poor channels, and because our listeners often do not understand what we say, *our* words *do* come back to us void because they have never really penetrated the people's hearts and minds.

However, if we have shared something that they are able to receive at an appropriate level then I believe that this is something that the Holy Spirit can continue to work on. And when either you or another Christian comes in contact with them later on, there is a good foundation for them to receive something more of God's wonderful story.

Conclusions

What we so often do as a church is have one idea, one event, one strategy, and we expect that we can both sow and reap in from that one idea. Later on in this book we will explore how we need different ideas and events linked together to make a sowing and reaping strategy.

Of course, this is also true of our personal relationships and acquaintances. One definition of evangelism that many of us seem to live by is that 'I have the truth and you don't, but you're about to receive it!' We see evangelism solely as an imparting of the truth, and we feel under pressure to deliver the whole gospel from Genesis to Revelation in one go.

Take time. Build relationships. Take people further along the Engles scale; further along in their understanding and receptiveness to the gospel. Allow the Holy Spirit to work on what you have said, while praying that they will come through to full conversion.

And that is true evangelism.

3

The process of evangelism

Just to recap, evangelism is a process and conversion is the end goal. Now we need to understand the nature of this process.

One of the most significant New Testament parables on evangelism is the one that is commonly referred to as the Parable of the Sower. Found in Matthew, Mark and Luke (the fact that it is in three gospels only underlines its importance), it is extremely important to look at if we are really going to understand the nature of conversion.

Here it is in the Matthew version:

> A sower went out to sow. And as he sowed, some seeds fell along the path, and the birds came and devoured them. Other seeds fell on rocky ground, where they had not much soil, and immediately they sprang up, since they had no depth of soil, but when the sun rose they were scorched; and since they had no root they withered away. Other seeds fell upon thorns, and the thorns grew up and choked them. Other seeds fell on good soil and brought forth grain, some a hundred-fold, some sixty, some thirty. He who has ears, let him hear (Matthew 13:3b–9).

How many of us in our evangelism have seen what is referred to in this parable as the 'rocky soil convert' – a person who believes for a moment but then falls away? I believe that the 'rocky soil convert' is the curse of the twentieth-century church – that which we put so much effort into yet for so little return. What we all long for is the 'good soil convert' – someone who not only remains personally committed, but who builds up the church through the new life he or she has received.

Let us look at Jesus' explanation of the parable:

> 'Hear then the parable of the sower. When any one hears the word of the kingdom and does not understand it, the evil one comes and snatches away what is sown in his heart; this is what was sown along the path. As for what was sown on rocky ground, this is he who hears the word and immediately receives it with joy; yet he has no root in himself, but endures for a while, and when tribulation or persecution arises on account of the word, immediately he falls away. As for what was sown among thorns, this is he who hears the word, but the cares of the world and the delight in riches choke the word, and it proves unfruitful. As for what was sown on good soil, this is he who hears the word and understands it; he indeed bears fruit, and yields, in one case a hundredfold, in another sixty, and in another thirty' (Matthew 13:18–23).

Looking both at this and the parable itself, a number of questions spring to mind. Firstly, what exactly makes the bad soil responses bad? (There are three bad soil responses: the seed that was sown on the path; the seed that was sown on rocky ground; and the seed that was sown among the thorns.)

Also, what makes the good soil good? To help us

answer both these questions we should take into account Luke 8:15: 'And as for that in the good soil, they are those who, hearing the word, hold it fast in an honest and good heart, and bring forth fruit with patience.'

Radical conclusions

So having looked at this passage, what is our conclusion? As I have asked this question to different groups of Christians around the country, I have heard many different conclusions, most of them agricultural in nature! But what did Jesus say? Verse 18 of the passage in Matthew tells us that when anyone hears the word of the kingdom and does not understand it, the evil one takes it away. Maybe this parable is actually about understanding, and the three bad soils refer to the levels of people's understanding:

- That which falls on the path represents people who understand nothing and are not interested at all.
- That which falls on the rocky soil represents people who understand something of the gospel message but do not understand the implications, and as soon as any difficulty comes from believing they fall away.
- And the third group is that which is sown among the thorns; the people represented here also understand a little of what the gospel means but they do not understand the lordship of Jesus. They do not realise that they may have to change their lifestyle.

If we look at the convert from the good soil we immediately see that this is somebody who hears the word and understands it – not only the benefits but the implications too. Then if we look at that verse in Luke 8 we see that the good soil convert is also someone who has an honest heart. The conclusion then is that the conditions for a good soil convert are honesty and understanding.

So let us try to apply this and perhaps draw some radical conclusions. Whose fault exactly is the rocky soil convert? In my own experience I have seen that when people fall away we tend to blame *them* because of their lack of commitment. But I want to make a challenging statement – perhaps it is *our* fault! Perhaps we have led these people to the Lord too soon! We have not checked up on what they do or do not understand, and are so keen to see people converted that we lead them to the Lord before finding this out.

See, it is possible for non-Christians to be honest about their needs, to recognise that they are feeling lost and have a life-controlling problem, and because of all this they say yes to Jesus. But they did not understand – because we failed to explain it to them – that conversion to Christianity is not some first-aid plaster, not some magical cure. Rather, it requires understanding not only of the wonderful benefits of forgiveness and healing, but also of the need for repentance and surrender; of the giving up of our own self-centredness.

Let me tell you, rocky soil converts are largely our fault and could so easily be avoided. If we actually made sure that these principles were understood, I believe that a lot of the disappointment that churches experience would be taken away.

A pastor called me a while ago and told me the result of a mission that had just been held in his church. He was euphoric about the 120 people who had come to know the Lord in the two-week mission. He explained to me with great joy how high everybody's morale was at how successful it had been. But instead of responding with equal enthusiasm, I expressed a great deal of doubt and concern, and made such disparaging comments as, 'Oh, I am very disappointed!' This rendered my pastor friend somewhat speechless and our conversation came to an abrupt end.

A few weeks later I rang him and asked how many of his converts were at his church that Sunday. It turned out that two were at church and the other 118 had disappeared altogether. Consequently, the morale of the church was now at rock bottom.

This story could be repeated again and again around the country, and all this sort of thing does is breed disappointment into the hearts of Christians. In turn, their energy levels for evangelism in the future are sapped away.

'Tell me more'

Let us think about this for a while. Those 118 people were obviously expressing something as they had prayed a prayer at the mission. But what were they really trying to do? I think what they meant by their prayers was that they would like to know more – that they were interested. By their actions, they were asking to be told more of what it might mean to be a Christian. But often the only response we have for this is to lead them in a quick prayer of salvation.

If we do this we must face up to the fact that if they make their decisions for Christ without sufficient understanding, they will be rocky soil converts. What so often happens with these people after they have fallen away is, firstly, that we in the church find it

33

difficult to relate to them because they have disappointed us. Secondly, when approached at a later time about Christianity, they may well say that they have tried it all before and it didn't work.

There are two practical issues for us here. One is that we ourselves must know how to lead people to the Lord properly – and we will explore this in a later chapter. The other is that we must train our teams properly and have realistic expectations for them.

Many of the missions that we organise are, to a large extent, sowing missions. They put us in contact with people who are at the lower end of the Engle scale. Primarily, these people have a negative picture of Christianity, and it is very unrealistic to expect them to understand in just one or two brief encounters what it really means to be a follower of Jesus. Therefore we need to have as a response to our mission things like the successful 'Alpha' and 'Just Looking' courses where people can find out more about the Christianity they're interested in. Once they understand a lot more, they can then make their decisions for Christ and are then much more likely to be good soil converts.

Back to the Engle scale

1 — 2 — 3 — 4 — 5 — 6 — 7 — 8 — 9 — 10

If we look at the Engle scale again, we can see that we have been talking about a process of understanding, from point one to point ten of the scale. Let us break this down into different sections (steps 1, 2 and 3; steps 4, 5 and 6; and so on) and ask ourselves what people need to understand. We'll begin with steps 1–3.

What are the basic things that people need to know? So often we presume that the content of the gospel is the first thing to communicate to them: that they are sinners, that God loves them, and so on. But I believe that they need to start with understanding certain characteristics of God, such as: God is good; he is alive; he has not just wound up the universe and left it, but is intimately involved.

They also need to know that Christians are all right; are not a bunch of fundamentalist maniacs; and that we are not hypocrites. (At least, most of us aren't!) That Christians can be pleasant people – in other words, they are OK.

So in our strategies of reaching our communities and our relationships with individuals, this is what we call the 'God is good and we're OK' phase. This first step that people need to take is called Sowing 1. The objective is to give people a clearer picture of who God really is. To take away their negative understanding of God and for them to begin to see that Christians are not boring, irrelevant hypocrites but genuine, hopefully caring people who have experienced the love of God.

Secondly, steps 4–6 are the content of the gospel. We call this stage Sowing 2. It is the basics of the gospel message: that humans have a problem, and that problem is our selfishness which separates us from God. But God has an answer: the death and resurrection of Jesus.

The third phase, steps 7–10, is called Reaping. At steps 7–8 we introduce the implications and cost of the gospel. Finally, steps 9–10 are about how to receive Jesus as Lord and King.

```
1 — 2 — 3    4 — 5 — 6      7 — 8 — 9 — 10
Sowing 1     Sowing 2         Reaping
```

Friends indeed

In the next few chapters we want to formulate these principles into practical strategies – for reaching both individuals and communities. But before we do that we need to look at one last important factor. If we're talking about a process of understanding, what is the most powerful dynamic that draws people along this process?

If you go to an average group of Christians and ask them how they came to know the Lord and what were the significant factors in that process, you will hear again and again that friendship with a Christian was the most significant one. I have conducted surveys amongst hundreds of different groups, and if you separate those who have come from non-Christian backgrounds and ask them whether friendship with a Christian was a significant part in their coming to know Christ, seventy per cent will respond in the affirmative. It was through that friendship that they saw that God was good and that Christians were OK. Then at some point they came into contact with the content of the gospel and responded to it.

The remaining thirty per cent came to know the Lord in lots of different ways. They may have been given a tract and responded to its message. They may have walked into a church for the first time, heard the gospel preached and given their lives to the Lord. They may have had dreams and visions of Jesus. As a result of their personal pain, they may have started asking God if he is really there. Perhaps through reading the Bible they gave their lives to Christ. Or maybe they heard a Christian radio programme or saw a Christian TV show, were contacted through a door-to-door visitation programme, heard someone preaching on the street or . . . dozens of other ways!

Thirty is a good-sized percentage, but I realised that in my own ministry, and that of many churches, we are concentrating most of our effort into the thirty per cent and are largely ignoring the most effective source of evangelism. Which, of course, is: plain, dynamic, everyday friendship!

The average Christian, when he or she is first converted, knows many non-Christians. But what so often happens is that month by month, year by year, this convert gets drawn into the Christian subculture. We are drawn into this subculture by many means. Perhaps the most common is by churches having too many meetings and expectations on members which restrict the amount of free time available. As time goes by, the new believer knows fewer and fewer non-Christians until reaching that wonderful point of sanctification – no non-Christian friends at all!

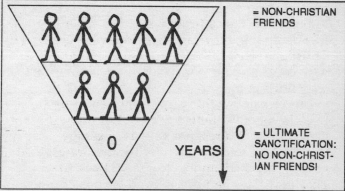

It is time for us, as the church, to break out of our ghettos and embrace the most dynamic form of evangelism – friendship – and to realise that the whole message of the gospel comes down to relationships: with God, with one another and, yes, relationships with the lost.

All of our evangelism – whether it is friendship evangelism, door-knocking, handing out tracts or caring for the poor and needy – needs to be from a relational perspective.

Can you relate to that?

4

Networking

In the previous three chapters we have laid the foundations that will enable us to start thinking of strategies, and to look closely at the two main methods of evangelism. The first of these methods can be called 'networking'. Basically, this is church members working with whom they have some form of existing relationship. 'Pioneering', the second form of evangelism, is where as a church or as individuals we develop a strategy to reach out to people with whom we have no existing relationship. And to 'pioneer', we think through how we might sow, reap and keep within that particular group.

In the ghetto

Let us begin by looking at this question of networking. And we should remind ourselves that the strategy we will develop will initially be one of sowing. Eventually this will lead to reaping and then to keeping.

As we have already outlined, Christians by and large have cut themselves off from outside relationships and are in the ghetto. Let us look at a simple illustration.

In the picture on p. 40 we see that all the dots in the square are folks in our community, and the Christians are represented by the picture of the church – *outside* the community. Our normal form of evangelism entails a few Christians getting themselves together and forming a posse or a raiding party. Then they see

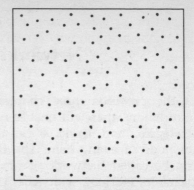

if they can catch a few sinners and take them back to their ghetto. Quite plainly, this does not work.

So why *have* Christians isolated and ghettoised themselves?

Some of the reason for this goes back to the holiness teaching from the last century. Many Christians became so afraid that they would be contaminated by the world – so afraid that new converts would slip back into a godless life – that in many areas of society they would withdraw. We see this in the arts and other media, but we also see it very much in terms of our community life. The church became everything we need in terms of relationships, and even today I believe that a fundamental reason why Christians do not get involved in relationships with non-Christians is because they are afraid of contamination and being tempted to backslide.

This is a fair point. But if we look back at what God has been doing in the church in the last ten to fifteen years, we can see that one area that has certainly improved is that of pastoring and accountability. Whether in the context of cell groups or on a one-to-one basis, there is more effective pastoring happening now than ever before. Think about it: perhaps the Holy Spirit has been emphasising this so that we can get to the position where we can go out and develop relationships with non-Christians. We can be strong enough not to be drawn into areas that we should not be a part of.

There will sometimes be occasions (but not as often as we fear) where our non-Christian friends are doing things that we clearly do not want to be involved in. We need at that point gracefully to jump out or suggest an alternative.

For example, I went out for dinner in London's West End with a number of non-Christian friends. We finished dinner at about midnight, and one of them suggested that for a little late-night entertainment we should descend on a nightclub nearby where there was 'a very good striptease act'. I knew that this was an activity that I could not get involved in, and I was frantically thinking of an alternative to suggest. Rather lamely, I eventually proposed that instead we should go back to someone's house for coffee. Much to my amazement everyone agreed. Obviously, we're still in the age of miracles!

So indeed, we must be prepared at times to bail out. But we must not let this fear hold back our commitment to make relationships and to get actively involved in our community wherever possible.

Reminders

As we look at this whole area of network relationships, let us pause and remind ourselves of a few things. We have already stated that seventy per cent of people who come to know the Lord make this commitment because they have a friend who knows the Lord. So networking and friendship-building is not an extra option – *it is imperative*. However, we can't just go out and 'be friendly'. If we were all to rush out on the streets and just be friendly with everyone, we would scare the local population to death! In our modern society this is just not feasible.

So we need to understand that all relationships and friendships are built in the context of something else. This means climbing out of our ghettos and getting involved with people through mostly non-church related pursuits, then building relationships from there.

In looking at the 'God is good and we're OK' stage, called Sowing 1, we can see that through natural relationships we take people along this stage. Later on we will look at Sowing 2 which is the content of the gospel, and at the third stage, Reaping.

Four areas

So how and where exactly can we build relationships with non-Christians?

CHURCH	SOCIAL RELATIONSHIPS
LEISURE TIME	PEOPLE WE WORK WITH

In this illustration we see that every individual has four main areas where there is the possibility of developing network-based friendships.

Firstly, there is church. Surprisingly enough, lots of non-Christians turn up at church for whatever reason. It may be through some other aspect of our evangelism strategy, or it might be out of curiosity. But it is important that our church is a friendly place where these guests are noticed and greeted, and perhaps someone will spend a little bit of time telling them about the church and how it can serve them. (It is also worth noting that in English culture we don't want to be over-friendly as that will immediately cause people to clam up.)

In one church I know they have set aside a group of people whose ministry is to welcome newcomers and strangers to the church and make them feel at home. These folks are called the 'Teddy Bears'. Through the friendships that develop, new people are added to this church every year.

The second area to look at is our social relationships – the contacts that we make in everyday life. People we meet at school, such as parents at the gate; shopkeepers; taxi drivers; neighbours; and more. Perhaps a good question to ask ourselves is: do we know the names of the people who live on either side of us, and above or below us? Do we know the people who live across the street? I know of one couple who moved into a new town and they didn't know any non-Christians there. So the wife got involved in the local Parent/Teacher Association, and very soon they both got to know a large circle of people through parties and events held by the PTA.

There are obviously many social opportunities we can pursue where we have shared experiences with non-Christians and by doing things together natural friendships develop. Through these friendships the objectives of Sowing 1 are achieved. But it is important to keep remembering the ground rules, that in these shared experiences we are not seeking to convert people – we are seeking to build genuine friendships where hopefully people will begin to change their picture of who Christians are and what they are like because they have got to know us. Also, they will hopefully begin to see that God is different from who they imagined.

The third, and one of the most dynamic areas we want to look at, is the use of our leisure time. It isn't a chore doing what we love to do, and we normally have plenty of energy to do those things we enjoy. When we see evangelism as a natural friendship process, as we have been suggesting, then we can do the things we most enjoy and still be involved in evangelism.

A lot of people ask why there aren't more men in our churches. Where are the men? The answer is that they are out doing all sorts of activities – such as playing sport – or are out with their friends in pubs and bars. So, if this is where the men are, we must get alongside them by getting involved in sports clubs and other activities. In these contacts we have a natural opportunity for people to find out that we are Christians, that we are not maniacs, and they can begin, hopefully, to change their picture of God. We would then be involved in a natural sowing process.

One couple in a very middle-class part of England were eager to get involved in evangelism. They could not see themselves out on the streets, but they asked themselves how they could use their home to build relationships with the people in their community. They enjoyed entertaining so they decided to hold regular dinner parties, mixing Christians and non-Christians. All the Christians were briefed not to Bible-bash, to be themselves, to be natural and only to answer questions on Christianity if they were raised. In this well-off part of the community from which the guests came, most other forms of evangelism had been ineffective. If you went door-knocking, the only thing likely to happen was a memorable encounter with a large, ferocious guard dog.

Anyway, on a regular basis many folks came to these dinner parties, including very successful professionals who lived in the area.

I attended one of these parties myself and sat next to a millionaire property developer who during the course of the meal asked me what I did for a living. I told him I was a missionary, then diverted the conversation by turning to the person next to me.

A little while later he asked me, 'Where are you a missionary – Africa?'

'No, England,' I replied.

He then made the normal response of, 'Aren't we all Christians here?'

Instead of answering this question, I pointed out to him that fewer than fourteen per cent of the population went to church. Therefore would he not agree that much of our population needed the Christian message? He did agree.

During the course of the evening we had a wonderful conversation. He did not give his life to Christ there and then, but he did move up the scale. And he said to me at the end of the evening, 'I am beginning to see Christians in a new light, and God in a different way.' Now, isn't that what it's all about?

The fourth and final area for network-based friendships is the people we work with. Obviously a great deal of time is spent with the people in our offices and work situations, so there is a great deal of opportunity for people to see, through our lifestyles and the words that we speak, that, yes we are

Christians, but we're not fundamentalist maniacs.

The problem with this area, though, is the growing trend in England that people do not work in the area where they live. Our local church is very unlikely to reap the benefits from this sowing. So, as local churches, we need to be positive about the building of relationships that people do in their workplace. Even though we may gain no direct benefit, we can see this as an unselfish use of our resources for the wider benefit of the body of Christ. We need to continue to encourage those in their workplaces that through their sowing activities others may reap in all sorts of ways.

Christians in the workplace

While on the subject of work, it is worth mentioning that in this area Christians have two commissions. One of these is their responsibility to be a verbal witness, in terms of letting people know they are Christians and seeking in terms of sowing and reaping to make an impact.

I remember as a young Christian in an office environment that I was very good at the words and was not afraid to speak of my faith. But I can clearly remember being in prayer at this time and asking God in what other ways I could be a witness. To my shame, I felt God answering that I should try working for once, that would surprise them! So our words and our actions must be consistent.

Of course, there are many on the opposite end of the spectrum who are happy to live the actions but reluctant to speak the words and personally identify themselves as Christians. This can be particularly difficult for some who are in senior positions. But I believe this is a challenge that all in the workplace must face, and we need to find ways where in an appropriate manner we can let people know of our faith.

The second commission for Christians in the workplace is the exhortation in Matthew 5 to be salt and light. I believe this is particularly relevant today, when a great number of evangelical believers in the workplace understand their faith in the context of their local church and at home, but once they get on the train or in their car they leave their Christian faith behind as they cannot see the relevance of it in the workplace.

It is essential that Christian business people should become 'salt and light', which means that they should seek to stand for the principles of the kingdom of God. We constantly need to ask ourselves how the values of the kingdom, in terms of honesty and integrity, work themselves out in our particular spheres. We have seen growing corruption within the workplace, so there is a terrific challenge for Christians to stand up for Christian values in this area.

Time for a recap

Let us recap where we are in terms of personal networking. We have begun to get out of our ghettos and build relationships with non-Christians in a natural context.

But we need also to go to the second stage – which we will call 'Sowing 2' – where we are introducing people to the content of the gospel. We will find that once we start initiating these processes, Sowing 1 (that is building relationships, 'God is good and we're OK'), is relatively easy, and the reaping stage is also relatively easy. But the hardest stage is the middle one: finding ways to introduce the content of the gospel to the people we know. This is the area that we should now take a look at.

Sowing 2

This is the area that local churches can help their members with by putting on events where the content of the gospel can be introduced. These events need to be culturally appropriate to their targeted audience, so obviously you would stage a different sort of event for different groups of people.

For example, if we were doing an event for 17–25-year-olds, we could put on a music concert where we'd ask Christian musicians to come and sing, and during the event they could drip-feed what they believe and why. Don't forget, the goal of this event is not to see people saved, but for them to catch hold of the content of the gospel in a positive atmosphere. Subsequently they can, if appropriate, be invited to an event that is geared more towards reaping. I know that in one area in Britain, many of the churches have grown because of putting on a regular evening event of this nature.

If we were aiming at the professionals that some in our churches know, the church could put on a meal in a restaurant – or as a group of churches in Luton did, hold a ball – where people are invited with a clear expectation that there will be a short after-dinner speech which will have some reference to Christianity. (There will be more examples like this in chapter 6.)

Another strategy that works on this principle, and that is catching on around England, is the Alpha course, developed by Holy Trinity Church, Brompton. This is a sowing/reaping strategy which is built around the question, 'Do you want to know more about Jesus?' Groups go through a ten-week course, which step-by-step raises and answers the questions that most people have about Christianity. Then, at the appropriate time, there is an opportunity for people to give their lives to Christ. (For more details of this course, see the resources list at the back of the book.)

Reaping

This is the final stage that the church can be involved in – where it puts on an event that gives people an opportunity to respond to the gospel. Such meetings were once called 'gospel services', but hopefully we can look at them now in a much more creative way. We should seek to put on a service that is seeker-friendly – in other words, a place where non-Christians can be challenged with the gospel but not put off by the culture of the Christian ghetto. We often forget what it is like to be someone who does not understand Christian-'speak', and forget how a non-Christian will view our particular service.

I am not asking churches to compromise the truth, but we need to put it across in such a way that it is not a hindrance or an embarrassment to our non-Christian visitors. Unfortunately, there have been many guest meetings that start with an hour of worship where all sorts of wonderful things happen which are not explained to the people present – be it the raising of hands, dancing in the aisles or manifestations of the gifts of the Spirit. After all this there might be an hour of preaching in the most vitriolic manner, which leaves our poor guests looking for the nearest exit so that they can calm themselves down!

To illustrate this point, there is the story of a young man who was seeking God and had been invited to a church service. Indeed, there was a great deal of enthusiasm and lively worship here, which he could just about cope with. At the end of the message the speaker invited those who wanted to meet with God to come forward. The eager young man was the second person in the altar queue. The minister in charge came and stood in front of a young girl before him and someone else stood behind her.

'Aah! Two-way prayer,' the young man said to himself.

At that point the minister raised his hands, cursed the young lady in a foreign language and she dropped dead in front of him (or so it would appear). Even though the young man wanted to meet his maker, he wasn't expecting to do it quite so quickly!

As the minister came to pray for him, he closed his eyes and prepared to die. As you can imagine, he was petrified. Fortunately, when prayed for he didn't perish or fall over. The minister then went on to pray for the rest of the altar line who were all affected as the young girl was. Later on, the young man noticed that the girl was wriggling, so perhaps she wasn't dead after all.

Now this phenomenon, called 'being slain in the Spirit', happens in many churches and there is nothing wrong with it. Being slain in the Spirit is where the presence of God is so intense that, in a positive way, it causes people gently to fall to the floor. But it certainly needs some explaining beforehand!

Another reason why Christians do not bring their friends along to guest services, is that they are so often embarrassed by what happens during them. This is the number one reason. So we need to learn to put on services that our congregations can have confidence in.

In one fast-growing church they put on a guest service purely for the existing congregation to show them what the real thing would be like. They promise them that all future guest services will be of that quality and nature. This is so that the members can have a confidence in that service – can know what is going to happen and feel comfortable in inviting their friends.

Willow Creek

One effective example we can follow is the Willow Creek model, which is a Sowing 2 strategy designed to put over the content of the gospel, developed by Bill Hybels of Willow Creek Community Church in Chicago. His strategy of church for the unchurched is a networking one, and he uses his Sunday services not as reaping events but as content events where he puts on services which are totally geared towards non-Christians. They are designed to put over the content and need of the gospel in a dynamic way. The church then gives people an opportunity to join a 'Just Looking' course where a fuller understanding of the gospel will be communicated. They have realised that a 'good soil' convert is one where both understanding and honesty are found in equal measure – honesty in wanting to follow God, but also understanding who he is.

There is a lot we can learn from the Willow Creek model. Let us as churches take this as a challenge to be sensitive to the needs of our community.

Networking and missions

The other way we can reap in the context of our networking strategy is to hold a specific reaping mission, or be part of a larger area mission.

Often missions have been criticised because even though a lot of people have responded, the actual percentages have at times been relatively small. Also, there tend to be a large number of rocky soil converts. However, these may not actually be the fault of the missions. If we do not understand that evangelism is a sowing and reaping process, we will not understand that missions can only reap what we have sown. In order that through our friendships people can see that God is good and we're OK, we find ways of introducing them to the content of the gospel and then bring them to the mission. There they will hopefully be reaped into the kingdom.

In this context missions are wonderful, but what so often happens is that we have not had a strategy of sowing and networking. Then, when the mission happens, we bring along a load of people who have not been through this process. They are too far down the Engle scale, and we expect it all to happen in that one meeting. This is obviously unrealistic, and if it does happen and they do respond there is a strong possibility that they have not really had an opportunity fully to understand the gospel and see that God is good. So they may well end up being rocky soil converts.

The other way we can use a mission is as a Sowing 2 strategy. In this case we will need to invite the same friend several times – once to hear the content of the gospel, and we can then discuss this with them; then at another point to respond to the gospel out of honesty and understanding.

In one large mission they saw a large number of conversions amongst the youth but a very disappointing response amongst the adults. Again, this is worth looking at. What do young people have that adults don't? The answer is, lots of non-Christian friends. So, in the meetings there was a huge percentage of non-Christians.

In the same mission the tent was equally full on the adult nights but mainly with Christians. The non-Christians who *were* there were very much at the beginning of the process. But this particular evangelist was being careful to reap in those who were ready and structured his messages accordingly.

Now, what could have been different? A year beforehand it should have been clearly understood amongst the participating churches in the area that this mission could only effectively reap what people had sown. Therefore, friendship evangelism/networking should have been the priority of the year, with strategies made accordingly.

In this mission, where they had a 5,000-seater tent, they did actually try to do this. But the reality is that they had far fewer people coming to the training sessions on friendship evangelism than the classes for counselling and leading people to the Lord. This should have told the organisers that they were going to have a problem. They literally had hundreds of people who were willing and waiting to reap people into the kingdom through counselling, but only a relatively small number who understood the priority of networking.

Indeed, at the end of this particular mission there was some disappointment. But it could have been avoided if there had been a far greater understanding and commitment to both sowing and reaping.

5

Strategies

In the previous chapter on networking we discussed in detail the concept of having strategies. Before we examine pioneer evangelism in the following chapter, let us look at what a strategy is and how it works.

As has been outlined previously, many churches may have an idea which comes from God, but they often have reaping expectations of sowing strategies and are therefore disappointed. The most common problem, though, is that there is no real comprehensive strategy on how an idea, whether it be a networking or pioneering one, is going to progress from sowing to reaping. There are obviously many ideas that can be used in reaching our community and we want to exercise as much creativity as possible, but it is important that we understand how these ideas work.

One idea that churches often use is the setting up of a mother and toddler group, which is by nature a sowing project – in other words, a pioneering idea in order to make relationships that the church might not normally have with mothers and toddlers within the locality. It is important that we have the right expectation for the right strategy, and the right expectation of a mother and toddler group is that it is what we will call a Sowing 1 strategy: a place where people can see that 'God is good and we're OK'.

What happens in many churches, however, is that they have a good idea like this and then try to do everything within that one context. So, they go in and seek to reap within this one event, expecting the mothers to fall beside their prams and be soundly converted. The problem of going in and reaping from this one event is that these mothers came along to a *mother and toddler group* – they did *not* come along to be preached at. Another problem is that within the one group you will have some who may indeed be very open, but others who have only just started to come and may feel quite violated by this sudden introduction to the gospel.

Therefore, we need to develop strategies where we seek to find out who is interested in hearing more and invite them into a situation where they *can* hear more.

Here is our planning tool:

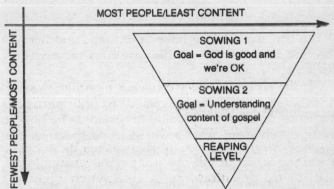

MOST PEOPLE/LEAST CONTENT

FEWEST PEOPLE/MOST CONTENT

SOWING 1
Goal = God is good and
we're OK

SOWING 2
Goal = Understanding
content of gospel

REAPING
LEVEL

All strategies work like this. In the first level of our strategy we want the most people and the least content – this is what we call Sowing 1 – and the simple goal is that people would see that God is good and we're OK. If we achieve that, we've succeeded.

As we go down the triangle, there are fewer people but there is more content. So the next level is called Sowing 2, and the goal is to put over the content of the gospel in an attractive way, but

55

there is no evangelistic appeal.

The third level has the least people and the most content, and this is the reaping level.

Let us go back to the idea of the mother and toddler group, and look at our triangle again:

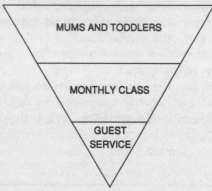

You can see that we have 'mums and toddlers' in the first level, which in this case runs on a weekly basis.

On the second level we have a monthly class on principles appropriately geared to the particular audience. In this case it could for example be how to bring up children from a Christian perspective. The goal is to find the people at level one whom the Holy Spirit has begun to touch, those who we have been praying for, and invite them to this level (e.g., the monthly meeting). In this context we can put over the content of the gospel.

Now what is important here is that people have made a choice to hear more, and it is very important in our strategies that they make their own choice to go from one level to another, so that they are not being violated and both we and they move with honesty and understanding. So we must make it clear in our invitation that level two has some Christian content to it. So if you had fifty mums in the group, you might get twelve to fifteen to come along to your next level, and this is excellent. Then, at an appropriate moment, some of these twelve to fifteen could be invited to your guest service. Five might come and two may respond to the gospel.

Now what is important in every strategy is that we keep all three levels running over a two-year period, because people will come down your strategy at totally different speeds, depending on the openness of their hearts to God, their circumstances, their backgrounds, and so on.

Let us look at this idea of strategy again by taking a networking strategy and following through with it on our triangle.

On level one of the triangle, or networking strategy, we have the 150 members of our congregation making friends through tennis clubs, barbecues, aerobics, parent/teacher associations, community action, and so on. As we have already outlined, the goal of this is Sowing 1 – for people to see through our relationship with them that God is good and we're OK.

The second level of our networking strategy could be to put on events that have a Christian content to them but are fun to go to. One area that is deserving of a whole chapter in itself is 'making the most of Christmas'. For example, if we had the resources, we could over the Christmas period develop a pantomime to invite parents and children to. Or we could put on a Christmas cabaret where we would invite our friends and there would be mince pies and refreshments to be munched during an evening's entertainment.

One church that did this had a Christian singer sing some Christian ballads, followed by a poetry reading, followed by some amusing sketches, and a speaker talking on the real meaning of Christmas. Then there were the traditional Christmas carols, and it all finished off with 'Rudolph the Red-Nosed Reindeer'! As people talked to friends afterwards they found that there had been a very positive response. In February, this particular church then put on a number of guest services in which people came to Christ and who are now a part of the fellowship.

So that particular triangle would look like this:

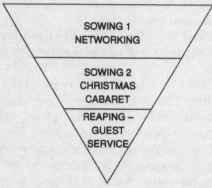

SOWING 1
NETWORKING

SOWING 2
CHRISTMAS
CABARET

REAPING –
GUEST
SERVICE

Another example of this is from a church where some of the home groups recognised that they had some strong relationships with non-Christians that they had been building. So they hired a room in a nearby restaurant and invited their friends, making it clear to them that there would be an after-dinner speaker talking on 'Is Christianity the answer to the problems of the world?' They had a very nice dinner in the restaurant, the after-dinner speaker spoke for no more than fifteen minutes, there were no prayers, and he made them laugh as well as saying some very meaningful things. The church members followed this up at a later date by inviting their friends to a guest service.

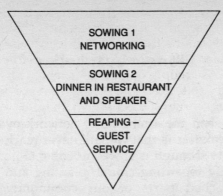

So that particular strategy would look like this.

In this case, the guest service had a tremendous effect on the husband of a Christian wife, and he came to know the Lord.

In our next chapter we will look at pioneer evangelism and examine many more instances of strategies.

6

Pioneer evangelism

We have seen the strengths of network evangelism. But its weakness is that we will never reach an entire community through it. If we are going to go forward, particularly regarding church planting and reaching the unreached parts of our community, pioneer evangelism must be on the agenda. Networking on its own would just take too long.

Our next heading then is obviously:

What is pioneer evangelism?

Pioneer strategies have three elements which make them different from networking. One is the reaching of individuals or groups in our community with whom we have had no previous contact.

Secondly, a pioneer strategy requires certain resources and cannot normally be done just by an individual on his or her own. A pioneer strategy must carry the backing and resources of a local church or group of churches.

Thirdly, a pioneer strategy should be designed in such a way that a few Christians can contact as many unreached people as possible (in other words, a multiplying effect is needed).

All pioneer strategies need to begin with prayer and research. There will be more about prayer in a further chapter, but first let us look at research.

Know your community

If we are going to have an effective pioneer strategy we need to know which types of people live in our community and in what proportion. This information can be found out through local county councils, access to surveys and census material, and from our own observations through driving round our communities.

Most communities will have similar sorts of people in them but obviously in different proportions. A typical community could look like this:

- Professionals
- Married couples
- Single parents
- Youth
- Children
- Members of ethnic communities
- Homeless
- Addicts
- People with special needs
- The rich
- The poor

And the list could go on.

As you can see, we probably need to have a different strategy for reaching the families who live in privately owned homes, to those who live in council houses. We will need different strategies for reaching single mums in comparison to families – and so on.

The dynamics of these strategies will be similar to our networking strategies in that they will have a sowing element. And this will be broken down as before into two parts: the first objective being to show that God is good and we're OK; then secondly, the content phase, Sowing 2, with the reaping and the keeping.

Where are we going to begin?

In our initial research stage we need to raise and answer some of the following questions:

1) Who lives in our community?
2) Who should we seek to reach first?
3) Are there any obvious felt needs of this community which we could meet in order to build bridges and show the love of Christ?

Finding out who is in our community is relatively simple. But the second stage is much more difficult: finding out who we should begin with. There are perhaps two approaches to this:

a) Revelation – we can simply pray and ask God, and we can begin from there. Fair enough, but as we have seen from Scripture God also guides by principle.
b) Principle – what resources do we have in terms of people and buildings, and do they lend themselves to the needs of any of the different groups within the community?

I will give some practical examples later.

Starting with people

The Bible says: 'pray therefore the Lord of the harvest to send out labourers into his harvest' (Matthew 9:38 and Luke 10:2). All good pioneer strategies begin with people – those who have a call from God to reach a specific area or group.

For instance, a number of years ago I was working with a church who were very happy to be involved in networking, but said that they really couldn't see themselves doing much pioneering as they didn't have any resources. Anyway, the leader was asked whether a meeting could be held and those who were interested in pioneer evangelism could come along.

During the meeting, we went round the room and asked a general question: 'Does anyone have a burden for a specific people group within this town?' Immediately a lady responded that she had a real heart for working mums and single parents, and she would love to run a mother and toddler group.

We asked her if she had the necessary qualifications and was prepared to take up the responsibility herself. She responded, 'Yes.' Then we asked the church leader whether she had the necessary character and skills to lead such a project – he said, 'Yes.' Finally we asked whether the church would help fund the project and whether they would make a room available in their new building. The answer to all of these questions was, 'Yes!'

During the course of this evening three new projects were launched. So, to the amazement of the church leader, he had people within his church who had the vision, character and skills. All they needed was the backing and releasing of their church.

Now there will obviously be times when individuals want to start a project and they are not mature enough and do not have the leadership skills or right character. In these cases we will have to lovingly put them off, but say to them that if and when they develop we would reconsider.

Perhaps it goes without saying then that as leaders in churches we must create the atmosphere and the opportunities for people to develop vision. Then we have to find ways to help them carry out that vision if it is appropriate and keep them accountable to the church.

Sometimes the vision may come from the leaders and an individual may respond to it. But it is important that we create churches that operate not only from top-down but bottom-up!

So people are a very important aspect of resources and an important indicator of the pioneer strategies with which we should begin.

Develop a strategy

Hopefully, either by revelation or by principle, or both, we have begun to decide on a particular group of people to which we want to reach out.

Now comes the developing of our strategy, where the individual or team that are seeking to work on this pioneering project must outline what their strategy should look like through prayer and research.

It would be helpful for them to have the three elements of sowing, reaping and keeping, before they begin. Even though in some cases it might be several years from the initial sowing through to seeing the end results, it is good to know where we are going before we begin.

Maybe it would be helpful now to look at some examples.

A strategy for older people

An Anglican church began to look at its community and found that the existing church members were mainly young families. But living in their parish there were a great many elderly folk who were not very well off, and the church realised they had not reached out to these people. So they began to develop a strategy, looking at their resources both in terms of buildings and people.

They had a curate who was very keen on leading this particular strategy, and the county council had just returned a building to the church which had once been a school. In this building was a commercial kitchen and a dining room. So they got together a team who prayed and they decided to hold a regular lunch club. Basically they looked at all the other clubs that were being held in the area and they put on a luncheon that was twice as good and half the price of anything else.

One hundred and thirty people came to their first lunch. Obviously, this was their 'God is good and we're OK' strategy. At the end of the lunch they had a short 'thought for the day' (modelled on the popular BBC radio feature). This was extremely brief and low key.

The church spent about six months allowing this phase to gain momentum and to win the trust and friendship of those who were coming. After this they would put on an occasional afternoon tea with a speaker of roughly the same background and age of those at the lunch club. The speaker would share some experience and adventure from his or her life and how Jesus had been real to them in that.

There were now 130 coming to the luncheon, and out of this about 40 started to come to the afternoon teas. After a period of time they invited some of those who came to the teas to come to church – eight came, and out of this two responded to Christ. Two from 130 may not sound many, but the other 128 did move along the scale for the next encounter.

If we put this into our planning triangle it would look like this:

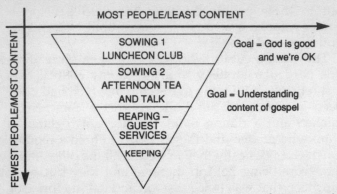

Once again it is important to notice in this scenario that we have the most people and least gospel content in the first phase, and fewer people and most gospel content in the subsequent phases.

It is also important to note that at each phase you give people the choice to 'come on down', so to speak – come on down the triangle! Our responsibility is to be praying and believing God to touch people and make them aware of him, and to offer people an opportunity to come to the next phase. At no point must individuals be violated; they should be hearing what they expect to hear and receiving what they expect to receive.

Again, a strategy like this will be most effective if it can run for at least two years. This is because people will come down the strategy at lots of different speeds.

Since we are genuinely concerned for people, each of the phases in this strategy is valid in its own right and must be maintained. Providing a good lunch club is valid for just that reason. We all appreciate good, cheap food!

Mothers and toddlers

Let us look at another area in our community: that of the pioneer strategy for mothers and toddlers (or, in our politically correct world, parent and child group). Again and again I have heard of these groups being closed down, and people running these groups feeling discouraged because they had not seen mothers falling to their knees on toy-strewn floors in repentance!

But all this disappointment can be so easily avoided. Let us look at this as a sowing and reaping strategy.

- Sowing 1 – the mother and toddler group, which is held on a regular weekly basis and provides an excellent service for the parents in that area. The objective, as mentioned before, is to show that God is good and we're OK.
- Sowing 2 – an afternoon, or a further coffee morning, where we put on a monthly talk on how to bring up children. It should be clearly stated that the speakers will talk from a Christian perspective. Alternatively, there are some excellent videos available that cover this type of material if we don't have access to speakers. Through these talks the content of the gospel can be slowly put across.

We may have forty adults in this group and twelve or thirteen will come along to our coffee mornings or monthly talks. Through this genuine friendship can be built, and then we can put out an invitation to those who would want to come to our guest services.

A church leader wrote to me recently to say that since the church had put up a strategy like this they had seen eight to ten mothers come to the Lord. Before this, they had run the same group but with no real results.

So, back to our planning triangle:

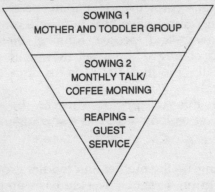

SOWING 1
MOTHER AND TODDLER GROUP

SOWING 2
MONTHLY TALK/
COFFEE MORNING

REAPING –
GUEST
SERVICE

Strategy for youth

Now let us look at a totally different age range: a pioneering strategy for youth. There are many examples from around the nation that we could look at, but here is one of a sowing, reaping and keeping strategy.

A youth worker who had been trained in these evangelism principles joined a church and became responsible for the youth work. He inherited a group of eighteen young people.

He spent the first six months with this group and introduced them to discipleship, the principles of the Lordship of Christ and what real commitment to Jesus is all about. At the end of the six months he had nine young people left – so far so bad!

These nine young people plus the youth worker had a desire to reach their community, so they began the process of prayer and research. They asked themselves: who should they reach out to, where *were* the people they were to reach out to, and how were they going to do it? These are the primary questions of a pioneering strategy.

Within their urban area there was a very large comprehensive school where most of the nine young people came from. Logically, they decided to focus on this.

Most of the young people at this time were into rave music. They had the use of an old church school and were able to paint it and do it up so that it would be suitable. Then they began to hold monthly raves. The youth worker knew a backslidden Christian who was a rave DJ, and he came and did the music for them. Over 200 young people were attracted each month. It was all secular music, and to all intents and purposes it was a secular event – but it was known that the Christian youth group was sponsoring it and the nine Christians were in the crowds making friends.

After a few raves the youth group introduced the second part of the strategy. This event was called the bin (short for dustbin) and was basically a forty-five minute discussion on a specific relevant theme for young people (the themes included loneliness, drugs, suicide and sex). The discussion would be a twenty-minute presentation, followed by the young people seeking to tear the Christian view apart. This would be followed by forty-five minutes of fun and skits.

So, when people left the rave they were invited to the bin, which was held on a weekly basis. Two hundred came to the rave and about 60 turned up regularly to the bin. After a while the young people were told that at the next bin they would be given an opportunity to respond to God – in other words, it would be a reaping bin.

During the previous weeks the people had heard what it would really be like to be a Christian and the cost had been laid out in no uncertain terms. So they knew that if they responded to Jesus it would mean a radical change in life style in terms of drugs and sex, and so on. In that first reaping bin over twenty people responded to Christ. They then all became part of the team and were involved in the raves and future bins.

This strategy was maintained over a two-year period and more than 150 young people, many from an unchurched background, had given their lives to Christ.

Now they no longer need to do their raves. They have moved on to networking – these 150 young people have several thousand unchurched friends who they can invite to the bin.

In this particular example, a separate keeping strategy needed to be thought through. There will be more of this in a later chapter, but it is very important that as much thought is given to the keeping strategy as to the sowing and reaping strategy. This is because it is more than likely that the people we are reaching may not fit in to our existing church structures.

Obviously if we are pioneering in a church-planting situation we will be making sure that the church we've planted is relevant to the people we are reaching. But if we are seeking to have these new converts amalgamate into an existing structure we may need to give this some special thought. It is the experience of many that people from a different cultural background, or a radically different age group, may bounce back out of our church again.

So we might as well never have pioneered in the first place. There is little point in winning people to Jesus, then losing them!

On the streets

Let us look now at how the principles of sowing and reaping might affect our approach to open-air evangelism and street work.

In recent years open-air evangelism has become more and more popular, and this is, of course, a positive thing. However, I have noticed that more and more street work has reaping as its aim – and more and more open-air evangelists are seeking for people to make decisions there and then on the streets.

What tends to happen at open-airs is that in our one-to-one conversations with individuals we give people the entire gospel message, regardless of whether they want to hear it or not. Unfortunately, more often than not, this leaves people feeling Bible bashed or violated.

It is interesting to note that the most fruitful open-air strategies are those that contain a number of different elements. One example is: a group goes out on the streets with their dramas and music, but the goal of their open-air is to make friends and invite people to their coffee bar. Those going out are encouraged not to feel under pressure to tell everyone they meet the entire gospel; rather, they are to find out where people are at and hopefully take them one or two steps further along the Engle scale. In other words, they are to leave people positive for the next Holy Spirit encounter.

The team are encouraged to make maybe one statement to the people they talk to as to why they are out on the streets, but from there on just to answer questions – and if the individual stops asking questions, to chat about the town or just make conversation. They are also encouraged to invite people along to the coffee bar where there will be music and an opportunity to hear more about Christianity. Then from the coffee bar people can be invited to things like special evangelistic events. This is a strategy for all – those who don't feel able to give the whole content of the gospel to a total stranger can do *this* without being embarrassed!

So, in terms of our planning triangle, this open-air strategy looks like this:

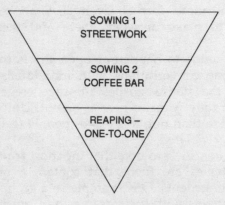

- Sowing 1 – Attractive open-airs with a friendship goal.
- Sowing 2 – A coffee bar or music concert with a group. This is an event where the content of the gospel will be explained. Musicians like Phil and John have specialised in a humorous and musical way of presenting the Christian message, without asking people to make a decision and in a cringe-free manner.
- Reaping – People being led to Christ on a one-to-one basis; inviting people to a guest service or evangelistic presentation.

When street work has been done like this it creates a much more positive environment within the town. It doesn't reinforce the stereotypes that people have of Christians and is on the whole far more effective than expecting people to respond there and then on the streets.

This does not mean that we must not preach on the streets – by all means do so. But let us preach with sowing in mind. We can talk about the needs of our society and how society cannot meet these needs, and then we can explain why Christ is the only answer. See, our preaching should not be about getting at people; it should identify a need that all of us have and show how Christ is the answer.

Summing up

In this chapter we have highlighted just a few pioneer strategies. At the end of the book a number of resources are listed where more examples of pioneer strategies can be obtained.

So in summary, all strategies, be they network or pioneering, are relational in nature.

All strategies need to meet people where they are at in terms of understanding who God is and what the Christian message is – then take them forward from there.

All strategies need to give people a free choice to hear more if they want.

And all strategies need to contain the three basic elements of the sowing and reaping process: Sowing 1, Sowing 2 and Reaping.

7

What is the gospel?

Having looked at some of the issues that relate to what evangelism is and how to plan a strategy, we need to ask ourselves: what exactly *is* the message that we are putting across and want people to understand?

Perhaps part of the reason we have so much discipleship to do, and part of the reason people seem to believe and then fall away, is that we are not really preaching the gospel. When asking Christians the question: 'What is the gospel?', you get some very interesting answers.

Basically, these answers focus on the benefits of the gospel: forgiveness, cleansing, eternal life, new life – and how the cross is linked to the benefits: Jesus died to give us these things. Only occasionally is there the mention of sin.

We would all agree that these benefits are true, yet is this the gospel message? We perhaps need to ask ourselves some difficult theological questions such as, 'What is sin?'

Maybe we should look at this in a fairly simple way, and make sure that the gospel message contains not only the benefits of the gospel but also deals with issues such as sin and repentance.

Sin and selfishness

As already hinted at in an earlier chapter, the problem with 'sin' is that it is a concept that is only barely understood by the average Christian, and hardly understood at all by the person on the street. So what term can we use that speaks forcibly into our culture about what sin is and isn't?

Maybe a word to consider is 'selfishness', along with the concept of self-centredness and the principle of self-rule. Whereas the average person struggles to understand the word sin, if you were to say to them, 'Do you think that the problems in former Yugoslavia have something to do with human and national selfishness?', there is no doubt that they would say, 'Yes.' If you were also to ask, 'Do you think that marriage break-ups have something to do with individual selfishness?', again you would get a positive response.

More personally still, if you were to ask the average person if they thought that selfishness was a problem in their lives, would we not find that a great many people in an honest moment would agree?

The start of it all

So, in biblical terms is there a correlation between the concept of selfishness and that of sin?

In the Book of Genesis we see two trees in the Garden of Eden. The first is the Tree of Life, symbolising a God-centred universe – that all that mankind needed to know about life, and right and wrong could be found in a relationship with God. Therefore, living under the tree is only good sense – it's the best for us, and it's what God intended. It was the purpose of God that we should live in a God-centred universe and in relationship with him.

However, mankind had another option – this was symbolised in the Tree of the Knowledge of Good and Evil. Here the choice was that mankind could partake of this tree and therefore put his own judgment at the centre of the universe. In other words, mankind would choose for itself what was right and wrong. This tree therefore symbolises a self-centred worldview: each person choosing for him or herself what is right and wrong, with selfishness at the centre of the universe.

It is not difficult to understand from God's perspective why the most severe consequences were attached to the possibility of a self-centred option. Those consequences are God's righteous judgment on sin and selfishness, and his righteous judgment means physical death and eternal separation from God. If we are in any doubt as to why, we only have to look at human history to know that we are not very good judges of what is right and wrong.

Again and again as a human race, both at national and personal levels, we think something is right when from God's perspective it is wrong. In extreme cases, we look at men like Hitler, Stalin, Pol Pot, and so on, who passionately believed they were right – that if you cleansed from society certain sorts of people (such as Jews or bourgeoisie) you could create a perfect society.

Now, of course, this is wrong. But we can see how often our own creature comforts, our own selfishness in fact, clouds our judgment on issues such as poverty, marriage break-ups and homelessness. And we can certainly see the desperate consequences of this in society today.

Two sides to the gospel

So from looking at it this way it is possible to understand that there are two major themes in the gospel message. Both of these need to be emphasised when the gospel is preached:

i) The consequences of our selfish actions – our sin – need forgiveness and cleansing.

ii) The death and resurrection of Jesus enables us to revert back to God's original plan, that through our surrender we place God – Christ – back in the centre of our lives and live under the Tree of Life.

We often see people repent of their sin but not actually deal with the principle of self-rule. We often emphasise the need for forgiveness and restoration but do not deal with the issue of surrender.

2 Corinthians 5:15 says: 'And he died for all, that those who live should no longer live for themselves but for him who died for them and was raised again' (NIV).

This verse talks about the issue of selfishness and self-centredness, showing that Christians should no longer be people who live for themselves. Christians should not choose for themselves what is right or wrong (i.e., the Tree of Knowledge of Good and Evil); they should surrender to God through Christ and live under the principle of the Tree of Life, finding out what is right and wrong from God's revealed word (the Scriptures).

Get the message?

So, as you can see, the gospel message should emphasise: the problem of selfishness; that we can be freed from it by surrendering to God through Christ; and that we can be forgiven for the consequence of our sin/selfishness through the cleansing blood of Jesus and his death and wonderful resurrection.

Now, isn't that an exciting message!

8

Leading people to the Lord

During the course of this book we have sought to take a look at some of the key issues that will enable our evangelism to be effective in the nineties.

But as we look back at the seventies and eighties we see that one of the hallmarks of evangelism then was that people believed for a moment, they prayed a prayer of salvation, but as far as one can tell they never really followed the Lord.

Again and again we find situations where in our enthusiasm we have led people to Jesus, but maybe these people were just saying that they wanted to know more. Unfortunately, our only response was to get them to pray a prayer.

Perhaps we need to ask ourselves some awkward questions, such as: do we lead people to the Lord too easily, too quickly? Also: are the means that we are using really effective?

In this chapter we want for a moment to tread on some traditional evangelical methods.

Honest understanding

Many of us have been using the popular sinners' prayer as the basic approach to leading people to Jesus, but I wonder if in the nineties this is really sufficient and if it was *ever* a good model for us.

We have said in previous chapters that, as we can see from the parable of the sower, a good soil convert is somebody who both understands and has an honest heart. It is very important in leading people to the Lord that these two criteria are actually there. We know that if people really understand in their hearts and are really honest it doesn't matter what they pray – God will respond!

So, when training people to lead others to the Lord, we should encourage them to ask sensible questions, such as: 'What do you think it means to be a Christian?'; 'How do you think this will change your life?'; and 'What differences do you think it will make?' The answers will give us some indication of how much an individual understands. If it is plain that the individual *doesn't* understand, we should agree to meet again later to *help* him or her understand. And encourage that person to join a 'Just Looking' group or Alpha course.

The content of the gospel

PROBLEM = Selfishness Sin
ANSWER = Jesus
RESPONSE = Surrender Confess
BENEFITS = Forgiveness

Let us remind ourselves of the content of the gospel so that we can ask questions that relate to these specific areas. There are perhaps four different areas that make up the content of the gospel.

Firstly, there is a problem: our separation from God; our selfishness; that we are living under the principle of self-rule. We experience this in our lives through the selfish acts that we do. Therefore, we can ask a person a question that relates to this – e.g., 'What do you understand about your separation from God?' We want people to see that it is not only their selfish acts that are the problem but the principle of self-rule.

The second thing we want people to understand is that there is a wonderful answer – through Jesus' death and resurrection; through his example; through all that he has done for us. Perhaps what we want people to see is how much God loves them – how much our selfishness has hurt God and others, and yet he has come to us to express his love and forgiveness. We want to ask questions like: 'How do we know that God really loves us?' or 'How do we know how to live?'

Thirdly, there is our response. Acts 3:19 says that we need to change our minds about who we are really going to live for – that we are going to surrender to God's love; be honest about our sins and confess them; and deal with the principle of self-rule through our surrender to Jesus.

Lastly, there are the eternal benefits of the gospel. We have been forgiven and cleansed; we have a relationship with the Father God; we have new purpose and direction; and on and on it goes.

Changing our minds

As already mentioned, in Acts 3:19 the Apostle Peter says that we need to repent and turn, and times of refreshing and cleansing will come from the Lord. Many of us as Christians see this word repentance as meaning a decision that we are turning *from* something *to* something. Therefore, we are very keen to get people to say a prayer as an indication that they want to turn and live another way.

However, this word 'repent' is the Greek word *metanoia*, which literally means 'to change our minds'. You see, real repentance actually begins in the mind and then manifests itself in our actions; we put our will behind that which we have already embraced in our understanding.

Many times as one counsels young Christians who are really struggling with one sin or another, we find that in one sense they want to follow Jesus, but they have not really changed their minds about their life styles. They still like their lust; they still like their immorality; there has not really been an embracing of God's view. And they have not seen themselves the way that God sees them: loved but still fallen.

So it is important in the conversion process that the fundamentals of what conversion is going to mean to them are covered.

Avoiding a cover-up

Let us look at this whole issue of honesty. When we ask people to pray a prayer that says, 'Father, forgive me for my sins', are we not perhaps indulging in a huge cover-up? Yes, God knows what their sins are and he longs to forgive people as they come to him, but so often even *we* don't really know what all our sins are.

In 1 John 1:9 it says that if we confess our sins he is faithful and just to forgive us and cleanse us. Perhaps it might be a better approach to say to people that there is much that God is going to do in their lives in the next few weeks and months, but to encourage them, as they surrender their lives to God, to take this opportunity to confess one or two things that they know are wrong.

One evangelist I was talking to told me it was his experience that he never had to tell people that what they had done was wrong – when they pray they know!

He shared a story of a very tough young man who unexpectedly responded in a meeting. So this evangelist took him aside to pray with him, and instead of leading the young man in the normal sinners' prayer, he asked him to tell God the things that he knew he had done wrong.

This young sixteen-year-old asked God to forgive him for the night he had grabbed and kicked and beaten an old lady. As he did so he began to weep and cry because he had just had a glimpse of how awful this really was and how extraordinary was God's love. As this young boy confessed this violence and surrendered his life to Jesus, he also experienced a wonderful sense of cleansing and forgiveness.

When people confess, it is an opportunity for them to change their minds. They begin to see their actions from God's perspective: that they were selfish or that they hurt people. This is no cosmetic cover-up – 'God, forgive me all my sins' – but a specific dealing with the selfishness that is in our hearts.

Jesus tells us a very interesting parable in Luke 7:41–43:

> 'A certain creditor had two debtors; one owed five hundred denarii, and the other fifty. When they could not pay, he forgave them both. Now which of them will love him more?'
>
> Simon answered, 'The one, I suppose, to whom he forgave more.'
>
> And he said to him, 'You have judged rightly.'

In this story Jesus asks the question: which one will love him more? Simon rightly says it is the one who has been forgiven most. Could it be that so often young Christians struggle to know whether God really loves them or not because they have no real sense of having been forgiven? When we truly confess our sins we get an appalling glance at the state of our own hearts. We get a picture of some of the really miserable and selfish things we have done. When we confess them and have that sense of God's forgiveness, a deep love should be born in our hearts for the Father God.

Could it not be true that we inadvertently cheat people by having them pray a generic prayer of forgiveness for *all* their sins, rather than getting them to confess those one or two areas that they know are wrong?

Another evangelist told me the story of a young boy coming forward for prayer to give his life to Jesus. The evangelist said to this young boy that as he surrendered his life to Jesus he should ask God to forgive him for something specifically that he knew he had done wrong.

The evangelist wondered what this ten-year-old would pray, but without hesitation the little boy asked God to forgive him for the bullet that he had stolen the day before at a show. This little boy did not need to be told that stealing bullets was wrong; the Holy Spirit brought his conviction and the boy not only gave his life to Jesus but had a wonderful sense of God's forgiveness. And he had begun the process of changing his mind about stealing.

When one reads the diaries of John Wesley it is very interesting to see that at times he spent up to two hours with people, talking and praying with them. For him, leading people to Jesus was not some 'get-it-over-quick' process at the end of a meeting, but a very genuine meeting with the heavenly Father.

So what are we saying? Don't lead people to the Lord at the end of meetings? Don't use a formal prayer? Not necessarily – but we *are* saying that there are limitations in a formal prayer. We are saying that in many cases, because of our enthusiasm or nervousness, we get people to pray a prayer when they don't really understand what they are doing. We are also saying that we want people to experience a real sense of forgiveness and therefore specific confession is necessary – this speaking out, or owning up to what we have done.

These may sound like radical ideas, but if we want to see radical converts in the nineties, if we want to see radical young people for Jesus, if we want to see adults whose lives are genuinely changed, then maybe we need to rethink our methods.

I surrender!

Perhaps we need to look at the whole issue of surrender. In the normal sinners' prayer surrender to God is covered in such terms as, 'Jesus, be my Lord and King'. But it is easy to say these words and not understand the underlying meaning.

Have a look at 2 Corinthians 5:15: 'And he died for all, that those who live might live no longer for themselves but for him who for their sake died and was raised.'

Here is a wonderful verse that shows that a Christian is somebody who no longer lives for him or herself but for him who died for us and was raised again. Perhaps we need to encourage people to pray a prayer that states in everyday language that they no longer want to live according to their own understanding of what is right and wrong; they no longer want their own self-interest as life's primary objective; and they surrender these things to God. They want to put him and his ways at the centre of their lives.

Addictive backgrounds

What we have said so far in this chapter covers most of the people we will lead to the Lord. But perhaps we need to think a little bit about people who come from a background of addictive behaviour and life-controlling habits.

With these sorts of people I think we need to understand that they are going to need a greater amount of ongoing care and help because they have well-ingrained, negative habit patterns which cannot be changed in a moment. Even though they can be forgiven and cleansed and have a sense of new power in a moment (the indwelling power of Christ), they still need ongoing help, accountability and care.

This sort of help needs to get to the roots of why this person has developed these life-controlling habits. There needs to be a process of honesty where the person identifies, often for the first time, what really hurt him or her and why – then asking forgiveness for the things that they have done and forgiving the people who have hurt them.

Next there is the process of changing the mind and building new habit patterns which are the opposites of the addictive behaviour. This starts with giving the person new values. For many people the most important new value is to see themselves in a new way: that they are in Christ and therefore significant, that they are loved by God and therefore valuable, and that they are created by God and therefore have purpose and gifts. As they see God and themselves in a new light there is a wonderful restoring process.

In a sense, all of us have to go through this process, but for most of us our habit patterns are not quite so negative and so life-controlling, so we go through this process on our own or in the normal context of church life and don't need special help.

It is, therefore, important that if we are working in these kinds of situations – and hopefully many of us will be – we need to make sure that either by linking up with other groups or through our own resources we have the capacity to help these people.

It is probably fair to say that if the addictive behaviour and life-controlling habits are strong, it will take between nine months and two years of fairly intensive care and accountability to see a full restoration where this person is strong enough to stand on his or her own in the context of a local church, a job and everyday life.

Summing up

In leading people to the Lord, maybe I can suggest a form of prayer that covers the following points:

- Firstly, a section that acknowledges that we have been self-centred but now we want to change our minds. We want to place God and Christ at the centre of our lives and turn away from pleasing ourselves to pleasing God.
- Secondly, a section that is the beginning of a process of confession where we confess one major area of our life that we know is wrong.

- Thirdly, to thank God for his forgiveness and cleansing.

Let us think through how we lead people to the Lord. Let us encourage our counsellors to make sure that there is real understanding, that individuals have come at least to a place of honesty concerning their own sins, and that there is a real surrender of their will and understanding to the Father God.

Then, and only then, will we see true, radical converts for the nineties.

9

Keeping strategies

As churches formulate their evangelism strategies, one of the most crucial questions they can ask is, 'Do we have a keeping strategy?' As Lionel Fletcher, an Anglican evangelist in the 1930s, said, 'All churches grow, but we must stop them leaking!'

A constant source of frustration is that even when the church seems to be effectively reaching people – even when there are converts who have thought through their decision and have made genuine responses – we seem so often to be unable to keep them.

Birds of a feather

There are a number of factors we can look at to help us overcome this problem. Firstly, as the saying goes, 'like attracts like'.

We have to face an uncomfortable sociological reality that most of our churches are fairly middle class. If we reach people who are similar to those we already have in our churches (in other words, if they come from a similar social and ethnic cultural grouping), then we stand a very good chance of winning them and keeping them. However, if there is a difference, we need to think seriously about how we are going to deal with that difference as part of our overall strategy.

A change in atmosphere

Another major factor which makes it difficult to keep people is that they often come to know the Lord in a certain sort of atmosphere where there is a lot of excitement. There are certain relationships involved, and the presentation has been culturally relevant to the individual. We then seek to draw him or her into the life of the church, where of course the atmosphere can be very different.

This can work both ways. People may have come to know the Lord in a very enthusiastic and vibrant environment. Then they come along to church and it is boring, unfriendly and they neither feel a part of it nor *want* to be a part.

But on the other hand, some people come to know the Lord from a relatively quiet process of friendship and networking. And they are brought into our extremely lively church services with dancing and loud music and celebration. This is equally culturally strange and sometimes very hard for people to grasp immediately. Consequently, they feel isolated and not a part of it all. So, understandably, they drop out.

Answers

Maybe we should look at some of the answers to the drop-out problem.

Church planting is obviously one of the major strategies that the church is using. When we plant a church we are almost by definition more culturally sensitive to the group of people we are trying to reach. We organise our church life and services in a way that is culturally relevant to that specific community. Therefore, we are much more likely to keep those people that we are reaching.

But in certain situations church planting is not an option for us. So what other options can we use? We know that the ideal is that our church is multi-racial, with rich and poor, young and old – and so on. But to get to that ideal we may need to take a step, a bridging step, that takes people from their initial decision into a group in which they can feel at ease. From there we can then facilitate them into the mainstream of the church.

For example, if we are a relatively middle-class church with very few young people, then we have a successful youth outreach amongst young people from a different cultural background, they will more than likely bounce straight back out again.

So we should definitely have a youth club which, in terms of its style and the ways that it does things, is relevant to those young people. We only ask of them a minimal attendance into the rest of church life, but over a period of time we assimilate them more. This type of strategy is commonly used with young people, but the challenge is to think about this for other age levels.

There are many Christian youth initiatives around the country which are attracting sizeable numbers of young people and are bringing them to the Lord. So, having an effective keeping strategy is essential. And of course, these converts should already know that discipleship is a key ingredient to being a Christian. When they said yes to Jesus, they should have understood that this implied a change of lifestyle.

Youth cell groups

There are many effective models being used for following up teenagers, and I want us to look here at a new and perhaps radical solution used by one or two groups. This is the concept of youth cell groups.

We have seen in the adult church how cell groups have been effective in pastoring and caring for people. But in very few places have these basic ideas been used for young people.

We know that historically John Wesley's revival was effective because at the heart of it were cell groups. In these 'single sex classes' as they were called, there was accountability, encouragement and discipling. In John Wesley's classes they asked three questions: 'What sins have you committed?', 'What temptations are you facing?', and 'What means of grace is God opening up to you?'

These three questions are at the heart of a good keeping strategy. They deal very much with the issues that people are facing, and in the last question the emphasis of the answer is not put on the cell group leader, nor on the structure, but on God. And those means of grace would include looking at the Scriptures, fellowship, the power of the indwelling Spirit, and so on.

Single-sex groups work well in youth culture. Cell groups with boys and girls together tend to end up with the boys giving their attention to winning the girls, and vice versa. In a single-sex scenario this complication is taken away and the whole thing becomes more real and serious.

With both girls' and guys' single-sex groups, there is a certain level of openness and honesty with which people are prepared to talk about their hang-ups, sins and other problems. In this situation they can receive advice and help from the group and group leaders. This also generates opportunities for the group to pray for each other and see God answering their prayers.

If we are going to have groups, the first question

we need to ask ourselves is: 'Who will the group leaders be?' In a number of situations it has worked very well to take the best of the seventeen to eighteen-year-olds and offer them training so that they can lead the cell groups.

In many youth groups, the bulk of the young people are fourteen to seventeen. This means that the older seventeen to eighteen-year-olds begin to feel surplus to requirements. So we can challenge them to take on responsibility. This gives them a real sense of significance; and it means that they are not just spectators in the group but have vital roles to play. It does wonders for their spiritual lives as they look after other people. And they will take more care to keep their own walk with God in good order.

Naturally, a certain amount of training will be required, but if these groups are quite small, then the level of training does not have to be too complicated. What *is* needed though is the overall youth leader to set a monthly programme for the cells. He or she should highlight a theme for the month and give the cell leaders suggested questions. They can use these in their groups to facilitate discussion and openness.

One pattern that has worked well is to have four meetings a month: two of these with a teaching/accountability emphasis; one just a social evening, an opportunity for the group to get to know each other better; and one where the group invite their non-Christian friends. This could just be an informal social evening, or involve a discussion on some aspect of Christianity. In this way the cells not only effectively keep and disciple the young converts but also enable them to reach out to their friends.

And so the network should keep on growing.

Retired people

Over at the other end of the spectrum, there are ways that a church can take care of an influx of retired people.

For example, in one church there were a sizeable number of elderly retired people who came to know the Lord and they found the normal Sunday services very lively and quite difficult to handle. So, firstly, the church created one afternoon meeting a week where the songs, fellowship and atmosphere were easier for them.

In this meeting it was also explained to the people that when they came to the main services they did not have to stand up all through the worship time. They could sit down when they wanted to without being frowned upon. In fact, one or two of the more lively people at the meetings were asked to lead the way by sitting down after a few songs. In other words, they encouraged an atmosphere where these folk could join in at a level where they were comfortable.

Relationships

Again and again we have seen that relationships are the key to being effective in evangelism, and they are also effective in our keeping strategies. Therefore, we should seek to bridge our new converts into relationships.

If we bear in mind the simple principle that we have already looked at, that all relationships are made in the context of something else, we must therefore create a context in which relationships can be built – in the main life of the church, and into our discipling processes. This ensures effective keeping.

Another important factor is that as we try, both in our network and pioneering, to have friendship as the emphasis, the people who have been involved in this process should maintain those friendships. This will help the keeping strategy. (In a pioneer strategy where we are using a small number of people to get to know a large number of people, obviously the personal relationships are not quite as strong as in networking strategies.)

There are some pioneer strategies where church planting is the goal. So here we will not have much of a keeping problem, because the church plant will obviously be culturally relevant to those people.

For example, in one situation a group had been working in the West End and had led to the Lord a group of people from the street scene. So their church plant was very 'street scene' in culture. These new converts fitted happily into this environment. That in itself has become a holding situation until they can be slowly introduced into a wider church-life context.

However, there are many contexts where we have pioneer strategies that are connected to an existing church. For example, there are the Alpha courses, missions, mother and toddler groups, social action projects, and so on. With these particular strategies we need to think more carefully about how people are going to be integrated into church life, as in all probability the people who have instigated these strategies will not have the personal capacity to follow these people up in terms of relationship. So we have the somewhat difficult task of introducing new relationships and new contexts to these new converts.

There are a number of effective strategies that churches are using that we may wish to consider. Some have successfully used a short course which introduces all new members to the church, regardless of whether they are new converts or established Christians who have just moved into the area. During the course, what the church believes about discipling and pastoring will be outlined.

These groups are normally quite small – seven or eight people – so a context for building effective relationships is created. These courses give people the chance to meet the key leaders of the church, to understand something of its vision and culture, and to review what they believe. So hopefully, by the end of the course, a new convert is known personally by name to the church leaders. This means there is a smooth transition from joining the church course into the ongoing structure.

Now there's only one thing left to say about keeping strategies: keep at it!

10

Prayer

Can we have an effective evangelism strategy, or reach our communities without prayer? The answer, most emphatically, is *'No!'*

I know that it is extremely difficult to organise effective, ongoing dynamic prayer in our churches. But if we are going to reach this nation, if we are going to take seriously the Dawn 2000 goal of planting 20,000 new churches by the year 2000, we must at a local level find ways of encouraging and maintaining our prayer lives.

There have been hundreds of books written about prayer – the theology of prayer, spiritual warfare and so on – in recent years. But in this chapter we want to take a practical look, and answer the question: 'Is it possible to have an effective, enthusiastic, ongoing prayer strategy?'

We are not going to go into a great exegesis on the importance of prayer. But if we go back to an earlier example, that of the parable of the sower, and we remember that we are looking to see the bad soil become the good soil, then we can understand that we must take the big rocks out of the ground and see some ploughing done so that the ground is ready for the seed. Our prayer strategy needs to be involved in finding out what the 'stones' represent and doing the ploughing in prayer as it were.

Having prepared the ground in prayer, we then want to look at supporting our sowing, reaping and keeping initiatives, and praying for the friends we are involved in networking with.

Groundwork

Firstly, we should look at preparing the general neighbourhood and how to identify possible 'rocks' in the area.

In Romans 6:16 we see the simple principle that we become the slaves to sin as we yield to it, and that individuals are in spiritual darkness, not only because of their fallen nature, but because of giving in to sin and temptation.

In other words, when an individual creates a habit-pattern that is ungodly, it has two dimensions to it. The first is that it is a habit-pattern in our minds – for example, if we have given in to anger over a period of time, that will become a lifestyle for us. If we have given in to sexual fantasies for a time, that will become a habit and a lifestyle too.

Secondly, these habit-patterns, according to Romans 6:16, have a spiritual dimension to them so that we become a slave to sin.

In the first illustration, we see a habit-pattern built up because of a series of actions. In the second one we see a padlock on this habit-pattern to symbolise the power of sin. So we can see that this habit-pattern is a stronghold in a person's life. If we can by observation or revelation identify these patterns or strongholds in a person's life, and pray against the spiritual blindness that they cause, then the person will obviously be more open to the gospel.

The same principle could apply when we look at neighbourhoods, communities and towns. If there is a particular lifestyle or response to life that is common to a great number of people within an area, then a corporate selfishness is taking place, a corporate habit-pattern of ungodly behaviour.

Now we see in the first illustration a build-up of a corporate habit-pattern which also comes under the principle of Romans 6:16. There is a spiritual power and stronghold that needs to be dealt with, be it materialism, fear, or another such attribute.

For example, Barry felt that he had the most ungodly father in the universe who was the least likely candidate for salvation. Every time he tried to talk about his faith or in any way bring Christianity into the situation, his father lost his cool and told Barry to shut up. Barry, who didn't live at home, was praying the general sort of prayers that we can pray for our relatives: 'God save my father, please move in his life', and so on.

After a while of this, he asked himself what the main hindrances were to his father being open to hearing something of the message of Jesus. In this particular case it did not take a lot of spiritual discernment to realise that anger was a major rock in his father's life. So Barry spent several weeks praying against the power of anger, until he began to feel that he had achieved something.

He then thought about the alcohol problem that was also evident in his father's life, so spent the next couple of months praying against this rock and the hold it had over his father. So the process carried on – with Barry specifically identifying possible rocks in his father's life and praying them out of the soil.

Nothing immediately seemed to happen, but about seven months later, Barry met a friend from his home town.

'Have you heard the news?' the friend said. 'Your father has given his life to the Lord.'

Barry was incredulous. What had transpired was that the local church leader who was new into the area had for some reason called on Barry's father. In the past, when anybody of a religious nature had turned up on his doorstep they would be blasted by great waves of verbal abuse. But on this particular occasion Barry's father invited the church leader in. When asked whether he would be interested in joining a class to learn more about Christianity with a view to adult baptism, he said yes.

At the end of this series of classes, Barry's father gave his life to the Lord. So we see in a personal case how we can pray specifically over the friends that we have in our network and how prayer can help prepare the ground. Then, when they come into contact with Christianity, they will be open.

Pray for pioneers

This principle can also be applied to our pioneer projects.

In the early seventies there was a YWAM group doing street work and pioneer evangelism in Brighton. But it was particularly ineffective.

As they enquired amongst other Christians in the town, they were told that Brighton was the hardest place in southern England for Christianity to flourish in. There were more witches per square centimetre, and 'people get saved in other towns on the coast but not in Brighton'.

So the team decided to pray. They also decided to do some historical research. One or two of the team members concentrated on this, while the others waited on the Lord to show them what the 'rocks' in Brighton's soil were.

Every Friday night they got together and prayed. And one Friday, the researchers came back excited at the identification of a major rock in the ground. They outlined how Brighton had initially been a very small fishing village, but once it was spotted by the Prince Regent the village was developed and enlarged into a town that became the focus of the pleasure-seeking of the rich and powerful. From that time onwards Brighton was the entertainment centre of the south. It is not difficult to see how the influence of pleasure-seeking and entertainment is a major rock that needs to be dealt with.

While the researchers shared this, those who had been waiting on God were gobsmacked because they had felt exactly the same thing in prayer. So for the next few months they prayed consistently against this particular influence.

There was no immediate change, but over a period of time, through their coffee bar work, they began to notice that they were leading more and more people to faith. Not only was their work growing but they were hearing stories of other churches in the area that were seeing breakthroughs.

Similarly, we can perhaps do a little historical research on our own town and neighbourhood. We can pray and ask God to show us how to pray for our area, and we can use our common sense and powers of observation to look round and see what influences could be possible rocks.

For example, if the neighbourhood is very affluent, it does not take a lot of imagination to realise that materialism is a rock that needs to be dealt with. Or if the area is rife with violence, fear could be a big problem.

How prayer works

Before looking at building our prayer strategy, one of the things we need to share with groups is a picture of how prayer works. We can of course do this through teaching from the Scriptures, but here is one modern-day illustration that could help.

Many young schoolboys have two-inch circumference magnifying glasses. These are not intended for looking through and enlarging objects; they have an altogether more sinister purpose! The boys wait for a bright sunny day, sit with their backs to the sun, take out their magnifying glasses and focus the sunlight through the glass onto some poor victim in front of them. They patiently wait, then after a while the victim will let out a mighty roar as the sun begins to burn into his or her neck!

Now what has happened here? Has the magnifying glass created more sun? No, it has focused the power and resource that is in the sun.

This is what happens when we pray. We don't enlarge God's love for people – God doesn't suddenly love them more – but through our prayers we focus God's love and power into the circumstances that we are praying for. So, every time a group of people come to pray, or we as individuals pray, we can see ourselves as that magnifying glass which, when held up to the sunlight, focuses the power of the sun. When we pray, we focus the power of God's love into those circumstances, to deal with the rocks and break up the ground, so that our ongoing strategy of sowing and reaping will be effective.

Revival

There has been a lot of talk about revival in recent years. But what *is* revival? Some people see it as God moving strongly to propel people into his kingdom.

But maybe revival is this: through our prayers the ground is so changed that the sowing and reaping process is speeded up. There are some parts of the world where the ground is so hard that when you sow you will reap very little. But there are wonderfully fertile areas in this world, and if you sow in them you will reap a good harvest very quickly – lots of people becoming Christians.

In a revival situation we still need to sow and reap, but we will be working in ground that will produce a dynamic and wonderful harvest.

A prayer strategy

Let us now look at a practical strategy for prayer. An important ingredient in this strategy is making prayer meetings themselves more effective. If we have a good idea of what to pray for, it really helps our prayer be focused and effective.

One obvious way of knowing what to pray for is common sense: simply looking at the things that we know. The other is to wait on God and ask for him to speak to us by his Spirit. In most groups we probably have a mixture of those who are happier with us outlining what to pray for, and those who are happier to wait on the Lord. This poses quite a dilemma, but I think that we can do both.

In our regular prayer meetings I suggest that we have the following slots for prayer:

We start with networking, so that every time we pray, we pray for our friendships with non-Christians. Pray that as a church, and for the people in the meeting, we can develop these friendships in a step-by-step way.

We then might want to pray for any events that the church is putting on that support our networking strategy (e.g., we might have an event that is Sowing 2 in nature where we are seeking to present the content of the gospel but not make an appeal).

We can pray for the mechanics of the meetings; for all the contributors; for the Holy Spirit to touch the meetings; and that people would come out of the events with a new understanding of what Christianity is.

If we are putting on a guest service, we should obviously pray for that – that Christians would have the confidence to bring their friends along; that the meeting will be led and planned well; and so on.

Having prayed for networking in our prayer meeting, we can then move on and look at our pioneer strategies. Our prayers will be at all sorts of levels. Some may be at the very basic level of praying for a person to get the vision for a particular project. In another situation we may have a strategy with a team involved – e.g., a mother and toddler group who are very much in the sowing phase – and we can pray for them. And there may be another pioneer strategy, such as youth work, where the organisers are about to put on a content event that needs prayer.

Lastly, we can have a revelation slot in our prayer meeting. In this we can ask God for any other agendas that we should pray into. There is a good chance that we will find ourselves praying for our nation or the world at large.

Prayer walking

Another prayer strategy that we can use is prayer walking. There are a number of excellent books that look at this subject in detail (for a list of these, see the resources section on page 126). Many people around the country are finding it extremely helpful to pray systematically over the streets and houses in their towns.

There are lots of ways that this can be organised. For a season, every other prayer meeting could be a prayer walk. Split up into twos and walk round the town, praying over specific streets that have been marked out for that evening.

Seasons of prayer

For many churches it is hard to sustain prayer meetings on an all-year-round basis. So they might want to think of having seasons of prayer.

Perhaps three times a year they could have a series of meetings devoted to prayer. All of these meetings could focus on our overall evangelism strategy, looking at all of its different stages.

The advantage of doing this in seasons is that for a short sharp burst they can probably get large numbers of people mobilised and involved. If they just have a weekly strategy, all year round, it tends to end up with only a few faithful people coming along each week.

All for prayer

As we will see in the chapter on leadership, the leaders of the church need to delegate as many tasks as possible, even prayer. So, it could be beneficial to have a prayer co-ordinator or team putting enthusiasm behind a church's prayer strategy.

But they must make sure that they are not the ones who are seen to be doing the praying. That way, everyone else stays at home because 'they' are praying.

We can all pray. We can all get involved.

Prayer for evangelism is for all of us.

11

Leadership

The role of leadership is crucial in any church's strategy to reach its community. There have been many good strategies in the past that have released and motivated people and are worthy and highly commendable. But the stark reality is that if the senior leaders of a church are not committed to a strategy for growth and don't put their weight behind that strategy, it is unlikely that their church will grow.

My research shows that churches that grow are churches where the leadership has said, 'We are here to reach our communities', and have fully backed the networking and pioneering strategies.

Are we saying then that these leaders should be *doing* the work? Not at all! The Book of Ephesians says that leaders are here to equip the saints to the work of ministry. In other words, good leadership is not necessarily doing the networking and pioneering, but rather creating the atmosphere in which they can be done effectively. Good leadership is recognising and releasing church members into the strategies, releasing finances, and being prepared to change church structures to facilitate the strategies.

Creating an atmosphere

Let us look at all this in more detail. Firstly: at atmosphere.

One of the fundamental things that we as leaders need to grapple with is creating an environment in which people can be released into their gifts and abilities. The Scriptures tell us to pray for the Lord of the harvest to send us labourers. As leaders, our labourers are the church members whom God has given us. We must empower them for the harvest field.

In terms of networking, one way we can do this is by taking some of the material in this book and sharing with them what evangelism really is, setting them free from their disappointments, and creating a new agenda in the church for friendship evangelism. We can share the simple principle that evangelism is a process.

We can also help to create space for them to make friends. In other words, we may have to face the issue that our programme is so busy with church meetings that there is hardly any time for people to form relationships with those outside the church. We will have to make some radical decisions if we are going to create time for people to build relationships.

When we look at the Book of Nehemiah we see a wonderful picture of a leader who created a positive atmosphere. His heart was burdened from chapter 1 onwards for the state of the city. Perhaps as leaders we need to ask God to give us a fresh burden for the lost; a fresh sense that selfishness is destroying the life of our nation and that we have the good news.

Also, Nehemiah had vision. He set an agenda; he created an atmosphere. We need to set that agenda and create that new vision that we are going to reach our community through sowing, through reaping, and by networking and pioneer evangelism.

In chapter 2 of Nehemiah it is interesting that it is the ordinary people who responded to Nehemiah's vision. They rose up to do the work and God blessed them in it. One part of creating an atmosphere is for the church members to realise that if their church is going to grow, if it is really going to reach the community, then *they* are the ones who must do the work – not just their leaders.

Then in Nehemiah chapter 3, we see the different groups building different sections of the wall and Nehemiah in the centre. He was not actually building the wall but was keeping an eye on the process. Where there were problems he would blow the trumpet and the people would rally to that part of the wall.

Release me

Having created the atmosphere, the second thing that we as leaders must do is release the people – into networking as we have already stated, but also into pioneering. We must believe that God is putting his calling into the lives of individuals and we need to find out who they are, particularly in relation to pioneer evangelism. As we have seen, pioneer evangelism always takes people and resources, and as leaders we must be involved in the decisions that have to be made.

But we create the atmosphere by saying: 'If you have a burden for a particular people then let us know.' The leadership team should then help to create a strategy that will make that particular project work.

Keep an eye out

It is crucial for us to keep an eye on the process. The law of human nature is that everything swerves to rot. Unless we are interacting all the time as a leadership team, our networking will peter out and our pioneer evangelism will get blocked up.

In the case of network evangelism, one church has found an effective way of keeping this alive.

Many churches in our country are fully committed to cell groups/house groups/home groups, or whatever you want to call them. But there is sometimes a frustration level with them, because they are so pastoral that often nothing seems to happen. We then cancel them and have 'interest' groups – for outsiders who are interested. These, naturally, are more outward in focus and so our pastoring suffers.

But in this one church, their home groups have two leaders. One is your normal pastoral, mature Christian who is a classic home church leader. The other is someone whose interest is evangelism. Once a month the evangelism person gets to lead the meeting, and basically he asks the members: 'How is your networking going?'

So in the group they go round, one after another, sharing their experiences. Some may say that they do not have any non-Christian friends, and the group should then seek to help these people out of their Christian ghetto. Or the individuals could look in their diaries to see how they can release some time for networking, and the group can pray for them in this.

Some might say that they are bringing a friend along to a content meeting (Sowing 2), and the group can pray for that. Others might say that they have made lots of friends but no one wants to go to any of the church's meetings. The group can then pray for and encourage them in the long haul.

Others might say they are taking a friend to a reaping meeting on Sunday and the group can focus its prayers on that.

Also, this evangelism leader could arrange for

events that support the friendships in the group.

So you can see that using your home groups in this way keeps networking on the agenda – once a month here it comes again. And this will continue to underline the fact that seventy per cent of people who come to know the Lord and aren't from a Christian background come through having a friend who knows Jesus.

Another way we could use this idea is to say to our existing group leaders, 'Could you make sure that networking is a regular subject within your house group?' This should not be too much effort for the main leaders, but it does keep networking on the agenda.

We can also use our home groups to get feedback. Did our last content meeting (Sowing 2) really work? Are there any suggestions? We can let our home groups know of future meetings, Alpha courses, reaping meetings, and so on.

And we should keep direction in our pioneer strategies. It is important to realise that people who are running a particular project, whether it be the youth club, mother and toddler group, or a caring project into the community, can lose perspective of where they are in the process. We need to check that they haven't got so caught up with the sowing that they have lost sight of reaping, and that they do have a strategy that goes from sowing to reaping. We also need to make sure they are not violating their strategies by seeking to reap from what is really a sowing idea.

Our pioneer people need to be encouraged as well. Sometimes it could take several years of sowing before they see any visible proof of God at work. Particularly in our inner city and urban areas, we need to be prepared for the long haul. Not every wonderful sowing, reaping and keeping strategy will work immediately. Regular encouragement is a vital ingredient to help these people keep going.

Finally, it is important that leaders make sure the prayer side of their strategy stays alive. To do this, there may be times when they need to call special seasons of prayer in the church.

Exceptions

Another aspect of leadership is understanding some of the exceptions to the process we have been talking about. Do things always work in the way we have been describing? The answer is no. Yes, most evangelism is a process, but there are definitely things that can cause the process to speed up.

For example, the supernatural. When we see the supernatural happen, perhaps in the form of a healing, or a dream or revelation in a person's life, that person is obviously in a sense catapulted along the process. But it is important to understand what this does and does not do.

We see in the ministry of Jesus that not everybody who was healed followed him; not everybody who was healed became a disciple. The supernatural speeds people from stage one to stage two – in other words, it convinces them that God is good and he is real (Sowing 1). But it may not give them a real understanding of the content of the gospel. So it is important that where we see the supernatural at work (and we certainly want to see a lot more of it) we take time to make sure that people have really understood what the gospel is all about.

Another thing that causes people to speed along the process is pain. When people are in pain they ask themselves fundamental questions like: 'What is life all about?' and 'Why am I here?' Having talked to many Mormons and Jehovah's Witnesses over the years, I am convinced these are the sorts of people they are looking for. They have worked out a little equation in their heads that for every 200 doors knocked on, they will find a certain number who are in pain.

Maybe the person is recently divorced, someone close has recently died, or something equally sad has happened in his or her life. And the Mormons or Jehovah's Witnesses have realised that these people are open and vulnerable.

I am not suggesting that we should all go out door-knocking, but it is worth thinking, both in our networking and pioneer strategies, that pain causes people to ask questions. And it is often the case that those in pain are most open to the gospel. God has called us to look after the orphans, the widows, the poor and the needy. These are the ones we especially need to show who God really is.

The third thing that causes our process to work faster is change. Sociologists have shown that whenever there is a major change in people's lives, they open up to things that they may not previously have been open to. For example, a lot of people when they go on holiday or emigrate to other countries, come to know the Lord. Even though they would not have been open to the gospel in their own cultural context, the change makes them open and they reassess their lives and what is happening around them.

One example of this was when the Cambodians were forced out of Cambodia into Thailand as refugees, and there were several hundred thousand of them in camps. Even though in their own nation they had been extremely resistant to the gospel and only a fraction were Christians, suddenly in these refugee camps thousands came to know Christ. These camps became an incubator and training base for future pastors and church leaders. Then, as they were re-patriated around the world, Cambodian churches were started.

Another example is found in Eastern Europe and the former Soviet Union. With the fall of communism there was a terrific openness to the gospel, and thousands have come to know Christ in a new way. (It is also worth noting, however, that this openness is not just to the gospel. It also applies, particularly in Eastern Europe, to pornography, magic and every other kind of evil.)

Important

So, leadership creates the atmosphere and is the catalyst to the growth process.

Remember, if our churches are going to have effective strategies and grow, the leadership must make their involvement a priority.

12

Go for it!

In this last chapter we want to encourage you to go for it. Design a strategy that suits your locality. Remember, an effective strategy is going to have ideas that are of a Sowing 1 nature (which is to show people that God is good, we are OK, to break new ground, the place where we make personal friendships).

Then you will need ideas of a Sowing 2 nature (these are ideas which incorporate the content of the gospel and people are invited from a Sowing 1 idea into a Sowing 2 idea. The goal of Sowing 2 is to hear and understand something of the content of the gospel).

And finally a means to Reap. This is where people have been involved in something that is Sowing 1 and Sowing 2. They are then invited into a place where they make a choice to come where they will be directly confronted with the gospel.

As outlined in previous chapters some ideas like Alpha and Just Looking are Sowing 2 ideas which have a Reaping conclusion.

In the rest of this chapter we have outlined some ideas that have been used successfully in many churches and we have labelled them Sowing 1, Sowing 2 and Reaping. These are some of the ideas that you can use to start your networking or pioneering strategy. Remember, networking is where you are making friends in the context of everyday life as your Sowing 1 and then inviting them to a Sowing idea or content event. Pioneering is where you have no existing relationships and you're seeking to go outside of your normal social context to reach a particular group of people.

Here once again is the planning triangle. So put your ideas into the triangle, think through your whole strategy from Sowing right the way through to Keeping and then, with much prayer, begin.

MOST PEOPLE/LEAST CONTENT

FEWEST PEOPLE/MOST CONTENT

SOWING 1
Goal = God is good and we're OK

SOWING 2
Goal = Understanding content of gospel

REAPING LEVEL

KEEPING

If you look at the triangle the general principle has Sowing 1 at the top which is the most people and the least content; people are then invited into Sowing 2 which is less people and more content and then finally into a Reaping situation which is most content and fewest people.

Sowing 1 ideas

Be ready to share at a practical level   A man became a Christian through the 'ministry' of a lawn-mower! His Christian neighbour offered the use of his powered machine to help him out. After about six weeks of this the man was so impressed that he started asking questions about the Christian life, and eventually made a commitment to follow Christ.

By sharing your resources you can actually show, and not just tell.

Find relaxed ways to introduce your networks to

115

your christian friends   Invite people round for dinner – a few Christians together with some non-Christian friends. The idea is to relax, be normal. Don't push your faith, don't hide your faith. Invariably church comes into the conversation. Be welcoming, and don't invite the kind of believers who will have a cardiac arrest if one of the unsaved group swears!

Don't turn the evening into a theological fight. One man said, 'I like talking to you a lot about God, because you don't get upset about it'.

Be thoughtful and supportive in times of stress 'Get well soon' cards can be a non-threatening statement of care. Drop into the hospital, take some fruit, offer to water neighbours' plants, keep an eye on the house when they have to be away, offer to be a telephone point of contact for relatives.

Hold a party for your neighbours   Hold a barbecue – and invite your neighbours. Take the initiative, invite that lady next door in for a coffee and a chat.

Join in with positive local events   Christians can be really good at asking everybody to be involved in *their* events while they show little interest in everything else that's going on locally. Good contacts can come from putting a float in the annual carnival though not necessarily with a Bible theme. As a result of this you will find conversations beginning – 'Oh yes, I saw your lot in the parade . . .'

Luncheon clubs   Help the elderly in your area. See 'The Caleb Approach' for ideas .

Victim support scheme   This would need commitment, as victims, of whatever type, need long-term consistent care. Contact your local police station for details.

Baby-sitting to support families under pressure
Helping with practical needs like baby-sitting can be invaluable. Have a request leaflet or helpline to identify needs and allocate help.

Give support for those suffering with alcohol or drug related problems   Provide opportunities for access to support groups and counselling. The Evangelical Alliance can give guidelines on drug and alcohol abuse.

Bereavement support scheme   Reach out in friendship. Look at possible longer-term emotional and practical needs. Provide access to support groups and counselling.

Support group for people with Aids   Resources are available from organisations like ACET.

Identify the homeless and provide practical help
Apart from the practical needs of food, clothing and 'roof' explore ways of dealing with underlying problems which may have led to homelessness. Assist with contact with the necessary government departments and helpful agencies.

Housing estates programme   At a time when the children will be around, in a place where you are clearly visible, make a joyful noise! Use fun, music, songs – especially ones with actions and drama to draw the children. Have some of your team visit the nearby homes with leaflets explaining who you are. This helps you meet parents, and deal with any suspicion about your motives. Give the children an invitation to other events in your church programme.

Family fun nights   Choose a time suitable for the maximum number of children to attend. Use active games, thinking games, and team games which involve children and adults together. Encourage 'spare' adults to partner children who are without a parent.

Mix in entertainment slots such as songs, drama, juggling. Simple dance can work well too. Have a break for food and drink. Give a short, sharp visual presentation of the gospel. Make information about other church activities related to families and children available.

Nursery or playgroups   For an on-going way of reaching unchurched children, consider providing a nursery or playgroup. In its first year a nursery in a needy area of southeast London has introduced twenty unchurched children to a Christian environment. Children love it, parents appreciate it and visiting professionals are impressed by it. A family has begun to attend the family service and house group because of it! This area of work responds to Scripture's injunction to care for widows and the fatherless.

School assemblies   At first these can seem very frightening – a hundred or more children, and all your responsibility! But be encouraged – whatever you do in your ten minute presentation is bound to be more interesting than the routine school assembly notices! A song, a simple drama and a 'thought provoker' are examples of what can fit. Make your presentation as visual as possible. Involving the children will greatly add to their interest. A ten minute assembly can be the beginning of an on-going relationship with the school. You can give the children a taste of living Christianity, and you will be recognised whenever you meet the children in the future.

Preaching and especially making appeals are not appropriate in state schools. Contact Scripture Union for further information.

Youth groups   Still an important vehicle to meet the needs of young people. They will give a sense of belonging, and an outlet for social activities and witness. Many of the following ideas will help youth groups to be both purposeful and effective.

Sporting teams   Enter local competitions or just play regularly. This will draw parents and help with contacts in the area.

Join clubs in the area   Youth, school, Scouts, Guides, sport – they all need Christians.

Community service   Investigate what charities and institutions are in your area. Youth group members could get involved in practical help and caring on a regular basis. This should be a long-term commitment.

Making friends   Young people know the local hang-outs of their peers. Go along and befriend them. It is best to go in twos and threes.

Multi-cultural activities   Where a number of your community use English as a second language, encourage them to attend language classes as a means of meeting other people in their situation. Start a club where the different cultures could share their memories, interest, recipes, etc.

Holiday evangelism   How about forming a team to go on holiday together with evangelism in mind? Caravanning in Britain or on the Continent, going on a SAGA holiday or helping with a beach mission are possible alternatives.

Church newspaper   Print a church newspaper. Include testimonies, stories and photos. Let these stories cover the different cultures and age-groups of the community. Perhaps review a few of the restaurants in your area. Point out some local parks or places of interest. State clearly that this newspaper comes from your church. Perhaps you have a professional writer who can take this on. Go for quality – this could not only be a resource for door-to-door but also for your open air outreach.

Church video   Make a video of services, testimonies etc. Offer the video 'door to door' then come back and collect it and ask for comments.

Welcome newcomers   When new people move into your area pay them a welcome visit. Ask if you can help them. Give them an information pack on the best schools and restaurants in that area, and on your church.

Street parties   Encourage people in your church to have a barbecue, or organise a street party and invite their neighbours. You could include a light programme of drama and songs from church members.

Questionnaire   This is a good way to get people talking as it does not seem threatening. Devise a questionnaire that will enable you to find out the social and spiritual climate of the area. This will help guide you in your prayers and will provide a base for future door-to-door work. These could also be used to stimulate conversations.

Conversation   Simply talk with people and build friendships. It is best to work in pairs – male and female. Apart from a simple 'Excuse me, could we talk with you about Jesus?', there are a range of conversation starters. Be relaxed and be prepared to listen. Don't take it personally if some don't want to talk, there will be many who will.

Surveys about beliefs or with a gospel theme open up non-threatening opportunities to talk about the Lord. Community surveys will provide prayer and action points. Offering literature helps make contact and can explain who you are, publicise coming events or be a more direct gospel message.

'Magazine shows'   An action-packed 'magazine show' for youth on a regular basis provides an opportunity for young Christians to meet in an atmosphere they find acceptable and up to date. It can help break down perceptions of the church and Christianity as boring and irrelevant to young people.

Summer holiday weeks   A summer holiday week consists of activities for children of all ages. The venue could be a marquee on a local recreation ground or a public building such as a school or village hall. Use a varied programme of events ranging from sports, arts and crafts to Bible worksheets. This is a great way of providing a practical service for your community and making contacts with families who otherwise might not be reached by your church.

Sowing 2 ideas

Capitalise on Christmas and Easter   People who wouldn't normally be seen dead in church are often willing to turn out at Easter or to see their five-year-old do an angel impersonation during the Christmas play. Why not have a sticker or an insert that could be put into Christmas cards, inviting people to a special event?

Start an Alpha or Just Looking group   Advertise a non-threatening group that will allow those interested to look at the claims of Jesus Christ. This is a Sowing 2 idea which also leads to Reaping.

Family services   These can be a fruitful evangelistic opportunity. The programme should contain a wide variety of short items of general interest around a general theme. All age-groups should be used in the programme. There should be visual impact and audience participation. Clear aims are essential. What do you want people to learn? How do you want them to respond?

Home-based events   A group of children could host this event in one of their homes. Design special invitation cards and name badges. Begin with a non-threatening game to help them relax and begin to trust one another. The idea is to introduce the children to Jesus using a special guest or some other focal point. There should be a time for questions and conversation. The children could have tea together.

Seasonal events   Special events like bonfire night and pancake day give the opportunity to introduce children to the friendship and fun there is among children who are Christians. Think of parties at Christmas and New Year. What about a 'Hallelujah' party to replace Hallowe'en? The event could include a short presentation of Jesus. It is important that the event is better than non-Christian alternatives.

Short-term clubs   A weekly club meeting over eight to ten weeks is a good alternative when long-term projects are difficult to maintain. A membership scheme will give the children the sense of belonging. Whatever the style of club have games and activities. Children like both continuity and surprise so do some activities the same each time, as well as new things. Beware of an 'epilogue-style' slot which makes Jesus seem separate from the fun and games. Instead, either mix praying, worshipping and teaching throughout the programme or set aside some evenings of the club to concentrate on these activities. Be sure to keep good discipline. This idea can also lead to Reaping.

Concerts   Organise a concert where a Christian group can share their faith through contemporary music. Alternatively keep your eyes open for those that are already happening and take friends along.

Schools   Get involved in a Christian Union, or start one up. Take opportunities to participate in school assemblies. Pray for the students and staff to know God. Organise special events and ask them along. Contact Scripture Union for further information. See comments under School Assemblies.

Youth churches   To draw in unchurched young people, who may find the usual church meeting inaccessible, the 'youth church' concept is an option. Using a fast-moving format and music, youth churches are introducing a new generation to commitment to Jesus. Experiment with different formats, venues and meeting times. Some youth churches use a nightclub venue – including videos, dance music and light shows – and meet at nine in the evening. Others are more rock based, or use the 'magazine show' approach.

While using such formats, the youth church should still be geared to making disciples and drawing young people to a commitment in the wider local church.

Christmas Cracker   Every year Great Britain imports vast quantities of tea and coffee from the Third World. In fact last year we drank enough cups of tea and coffee to fill 40,000 public swimming pools! But though we pay a high price for our cuppa, it's well known that only a very small percentage of that price benefits the poor who produce the drinks we enjoy.

This Christmas why not get involved with Christmas Cracker's latest project. Has your church youth group run a Crackerteria? A Crackerteria is a Christmas Cracker cafe serving 'fairly traded' tea and coffee. But not only do Cracker pay a fair price to the growers in the first place; on top of that the funds raised through the price your customers pay will also end up back in the tea and coffee-producing countries where our help is so desperately needed.

Christmas Cracker, organised by the Oasis Trust and Alpha Magazine is designed to give young people from churches all over Great Britain the opportunity of putting their faith into action as they work to meet the needs of the world's poor and demonstrate that being a Christian can make a difference to the way they live.

And don't forget that because your Crackerteria can be open for the whole month of December or for as long or as short a part of that time period as you can manage, your youth group, however small or large, can be a part of the project this year.

(For more information contact; Christmas Cracker, Cornerstone House, Ethel Street, Birmingham B2 4BG.)

Mid-week service   This could be in the church building or someone's house. Use songs and hymns older people would enjoy. This meeting would be particularly suitable for older church members to invite their friends to.

Public meetings   Arrange a public meeting and invite older Christians to speak about what they have been doing and what being a Christian has meant to them. Their wisdom and the experiences they will share with their audience will be very valuable. Encourage the church to bring their older friends along. (Suitable Sowing 2 strategy for elderly people.)

Special services – Christmas, Easter, Harvest Have a Christmas carol service each year and invite the people you have contacted in the past twelve months. During the service present the gospel message in an attractive but penetrating way. You could use specially prepared invitations.

Produce a cassette for distribution around your area This could include testimonies and music together with an explanation of who you are and when and where you meet. A contact phone number for enquiries or requests for practical help or prayer is essential.

Street discussion group   You could set up a discussion group for those people in a particular street or group of streets who have shown an interest in Christianity, or are in need of friendship.

Golden oldies   Hymn-singing evening. Limit the choice to old hymns only. This is a good means of outreach to older people.

Reaping ideas

When it comes to Reaping we are basically talking about a small number of simple ideas that can be applied in lots of different ways. Some dressed up in a youth culture, some suitable for families, etc.

1 **One to one.**
2 **Inclusion of an Alpha or Just Looking course.**
3 **Some form of guest meeting** in a local church where people are asked directly to make a response or to join an Alpha or Just Looking course where they will ultimately again be asked to make a response.
4 **A mission** where, as a church or group of churches, we may have a special event or series of events in a big tent or hall where a well-known evangelist preaches to a conclusion and we invite all our Sowing 2 contacts to those reaping events.
5 **A week or a weekend away** has proved, over the last 100 years, to be an extremely effective way to reap. Whether it's a summer camp with young people or a weekend away at a conference centre with adults, getting people out of their own environment, into a place where there is a little more time to think and in that context provide a challenge, has proved to be very effective.

Resources

Books and tapes

Adams, Peter, *Preparing for Battle* (Kingsway).
Aldrich, Joseph C., *Gentle Persuasion* (Marshall Pickering).
Allen, John, *Just Looking* (Bible Society).
Beckett, Fran, *Called to Action* (Fount).
Botting, Michael, *Christians in Retirement* (Grove Books).
Briscoe, Jill, *I Caught a Little Big Fish* (Crossway Books). (Sharing the gospel with your own children.)
Burton-Jones, Julia, *From Generation to Generation* (Jubilee Centre Publications).
Chalke, Steve, *The Christian Youth Manual* (Kingsway).
——, *Good Questions* (Scripture Union). (An excellent evangelistic cassette to loan or give away.)
Collins, Phil, *Christian Growth Tapes on Streetwork* (available from: Youth Alive Ministries, PO Box 7, Bedworth, Nuneaton, Warwickshire CV12 9NW. Tel: 01203 643415).
Constant, Audrey, *Cassie* (Scripture Union).
Creber, Arthur, *New Approaches to Ministry with Older People* (Grove Books).
Dawson, John, *Taking our Cities for God* (Word Publishers).
Dixon, Patricia, *Aids and Young People* (Kingsway).
Earwicker, John, *Prayer Pacesetting* (Scripture Union).
Eastman, Dicks, *The Hour that Changed the World* (Bridge Publishing UK).
Eddison, John, *The Last Lap* (Kingsway).
Ellis, Roger, *The Occult and Young People* (Kingsway).
Ellis Roger and Roger Mitchell, *Radical Church Planting* (Crossway Books).
Finney, John, *Finding Faith Today* (Bible Society).
Frost, Rob, *Pilgrims* (Kingsway).
Gaukroger, Janet, *Sharing Jesus with Under-Fives* (Crossway Books).

126

Gaukroger, Steve, *It Makes Sense* (Scripture Union).

Gilbert, Pete, *The Teenage Survival Kit* (Kingsway).

Goodfellow, John and Andy Butcher, *Streetwise* (Kingsway).

Gumbel, Nicky, *Why Jesus*; *Questions of Life*; *Searching Issues*; *A Life Worth Living*; *Tell Others – The Alpha Initiative* (all from Alpha Products). (Cassette tapes, videos, manuals, worship resources available via Alpha Hotline 01345 581278.

Hatton, John, *Family Evangelism* (Scripture Union).

Heley, Veronica, *Hawkeye Hits the Jackpot* (Scripture Union).

Hopkins, Bob (ed.), *Planting New Churches* (Eagle).

Houghton, John and Graham Kendrick, *Prayer Walking* (Kingsway).

Hubbard, Richard, *Taking Children Seriously: Developing Children's Ministry in Your Church* (HarperCollins).

Ishmael, *Angels with Dirty Faces* (Kingsway).

Johnstone, Patrick, *Operation World* (Send the Light).

Knox, Grahame, *Drugs and Young People* (Kingsway).

Little, Paul, *How to Give Away Your Faith* (IVP).

Manley Pippert, Rebecca, *Out of the Salt Shaker* (IVP).

McCloughry, Roy, *Eye of the Needle* (IVP).

McClung, Floyd, *Spirits of the City* (Kingsway).

McGrath, Alistair, *Explaining Your Faith Without Losing Your Friends* (IVP).

McPhee, Arthur, *Friendship Evangelism* (Kingsway).

Miller, Paul, *The Reluctant Evangelist* (Kingsway).

Mills, Brian, *Three Times Three Equals Twelve* (Kingsway).

Mohabir, Philip, *Building Bridges* (Hodder and Stoughton).

Morris, Mike and Katey, *Pathways in Prayer* (Crusade for Worldwide Revival).

——, *Praying Together* (Kingsway).

Peterson, Jim, *Evangelism as a Life Style* (Nav Press).

Pierson, Lance, *Sex and You* (Kingsway).

Robinson, Martin and Christine Stuart, *Planting Tomorrow's Churches Today* (Monarch).

Ross, Alistair, *Helping the Depressed* (Kingsway).

Sanders, J. Oswald, *Enjoying Growing Old* (Kingsway).

Sherrer, Quin, *How to Pray for Your Children* (Kingsway).

Sprenger, Mike, *How to Present Jesus in the Open Air* (Word Publishers).

Thompson, Mollie, *A Letter from Emma* (Scripture Union).

Tournier, Paul, *Learning to Grow Old* (Highland Christian Classics).

Wooderson, Michael, *Good News Down Your Street Toolkit* (Lion Publishing).

Organisations

Aids, Care, Education and Training (ACET), PO Box 1323, London W5 5TF. Tel: 0181 840 7879

Baptist Union, Mission Department, Baptist House, PO Box 44, 129 Broadway, Didcot, Oxfordshire OX11 8RT.

Campaigners, Campaigner House, St Mark's Close, Colney Heath, Nr St Albans, Herts AL4 0NQ. Tel: 01727 24065.

Care Trust, 53 Romney Street, Westminster, London SW1P 3RF. Tel: 0171 233 0455.

Church Pastoral Aid Society, Athena Drive, Tachbrook Park, Warwick CV34 6BR.

Crusaders, 2 Romeland Hill, St Albans, Herts AL3 4ET. Tel: 01727 55422.

Evangelical Missionary Alliance, Whitfield House, 186 Kennington Park Road, London SE11 4BT. Tel: 0171 735 0421.

Every Home for Christ, Unit C, 41 Dace Road, London E3 2NG. Tel: 0181 9867114.

Open Air Campaigners, 102 Dukes Avenue, Muswell Hill, London N10 2QA. Tel: 0181 444 5254.

Scripture Union, 130 City Road, London EC1V 2NJ. Tel: 0171 250 1966.

Shaftesbury Society, 18–20 Kingston Road, South Wimbledon, London SW19 1JZ. Tel: 0181 542 5550.

The Glorie Company, PO Box 828, Rustington, Littlehampton, West Sussex BN16 3NS. Tel: 01903 783382.

There is Hope, 12 Montpelier Park, Edinburgh, EH10 4NJ. Tel: 0131 229 0003).

Youth With A Mission, Highfield Oval, Ambrose Lane, Harpenden, Herts, AL5 4BX.